BARRON'S BOOK NOTES

JOHANN WOLFGANG VON GOETHE'S

Faust:
Parts I and II

BY
Ruth Mitchell

SERIES COORDINATOR
Murray Bromberg
Principal, Wang High School of Queens
Holliswood, New York

Past President
High School Principals Association of New York City

BARRON'S EDUCATIONAL SERIES, INC.
Woodbury, New York • London • Toronto • Sydney

ACKNOWLEDGMENTS

Our thanks to Milton Katz and Julius Liebb for their contribution to the *Book Notes* series.

All inquiries should be addressed to:
Barron's Educational Series, Inc.
113 Crossways Park Drive
Woodbury, New York 11797

Library of Congress Catalog Card No. 85-4057

International Standard Book No. 0-7641-9109-8

Library of Congress Cataloging in Publication Data
Mitchell, Ruth.
 Johann Wolfgang von Goethe's Faust, parts I and II.

 (Barron's book notes)
 Bibliography: p. 121
 Summary: A guide to reading "Faust" with a critical
and appreciative mind. Includes background on the
author's life and times, sample tests, term paper
suggestions, and a reading list.
 1. Goethe, Johann Wolfgang von, 1749–1832. Faust.
[1. Goethe, Johann Wolfgang von, 1749–1832. Faust.
2. German literature—History and criticism] I. Title.
II. Series.
PT1925.M57 1985   832'.6   85-4057
ISBN 0-7641-9109-8

PRINTED IN THE UNITED STATES OF AMERICA

567   550   987654321

CONTENTS

HOW TO USE THIS BOOK

You have to know how to approach literature in order to get the most out of it. This *Barron's Book Notes* volume follows a plan based on methods used by some of the best students to read a work of literature.

Begin with the guide's section on the author's life and times. As you read, try to form a clear picture of the author's personality, circumstances, and motives for writing the work. This background usually will make it easier for you to hear the author's tone of voice, and follow where the author is heading.

Then go over the rest of the introductory material—such sections as those on the plot, characters, setting, themes, and style of the work. Underline, or write down in your notebook, particular things to watch for, such as contrasts between characters and repeated literary devices. At this point, you may want to develop a system of symbols to use in marking your text as you read. (Of course, you should only mark up a book you own, not one that belongs to another person or a school.) Perhaps you will want to use a different letter for each character's name, a different number for each major theme of the book, a different color for each important symbol or literary device. Be prepared to mark up the pages of your book as you read. Put your marks in the margins so you can find them again easily.

Now comes the moment you've been waiting for—the time to start reading the work of literature. You may want to put aside your *Barron's Book Notes* volume until you've read the work all the way through. Or you may want to alternate, reading the *Book Notes* analysis of each section as soon as you have finished reading the corresponding part of the original. Before you move on, reread crucial passages you don't fully understand. (Don't take this guide's analysis for granted—make up your own mind as to what the work means.)

Once you've finished the whole work of literature, you may want to review it right away, so you can firm up your ideas about what it means. You may want to leaf through the book concentrating on passages you marked in reference to one character or one theme. This is also a good time to reread the *Book Notes* introductory material, which pulls together insights on specific topics.

When it comes time to prepare for a test or to write a paper, you'll already have formed ideas about the work. You'll be able to go back through it, refreshing your memory as to the author's exact words and perspective, so that you can support your opinions with evidence drawn straight from the work. Patterns will emerge, and ideas will fall into place; your essay question or term paper will almost write itself. Give yourself a dry run with one of the sample tests in the guide. These tests present both multiple-choice and essay questions. An accompanying section gives answers to the multiple-choice questions as well as suggestions for writing the essays. If you have to select a term paper topic, you may choose one from the list of suggestions in this book. This guide also provides you with a reading list, to help you when you start research for a term paper, and a selection of provocative comments by critics, to spark your thinking before you write.

THE AUTHOR
AND HIS TIMES

Faust and its author, Johann Wolfgang von Goethe, developed side by side. The work is not an autobiography, but it reflects Goethe's intellectual development. (Goethe did write an autobiography, called *Poetry and Truth*, about his early life.) He began *Faust* when he was in his twenties, continued it at intervals—sometimes neglecting it for years at a time—until his seventies—and then worked intensively on it until just before his death, at eighty-two.

When you hear the name "Faust," you probably think of the story of a man who sells his soul to the Devil in return for supernatural powers. It's a story that depends on the Christian tradition for its plot, for Faust is a learned man who wants to know more than God allows man to know, and to gain superior knowledge, Faust makes a bargain with the Devil. Faust enjoys magical powers for many years, is entertained by an emperor, and lives with the most beautiful woman in the world, Helen of Troy. In the end, however, he has to go down to Hell with the Devil, who comes to claim Faust's soul, in accordance with their bargain. This traditional Faust story is a Christian cautionary tale—it warns that you will lose your eternal soul if you try to outsmart God. It's also a German story. There was a real Dr. Faustus, who lived in Wittenberg in the fifteenth century, but the truth about his life is impossible to disentangle from the legend. The

Faust legend has been used by many writers, including Christopher Marlowe, whose *Doctor Faustus* was published in the early seventeenth century.

Goethe's *Faust* is very different from other Faust stories. His *Faust* is sometimes seen as opening up a whole new era of Western thought. Modern people, say some writers, have been cut adrift and are wandering aimlessly in a technological world, searching for meaning in life and striving for fulfillment. In previous eras people could find meaning and achieve salvation through religion. In the West it was through Christianity. But Faust, these writers assert, achieved his own salvation through action.

Goethe was born into a well-to-do family in Frankfurt am Main, Germany in 1749, in the middle of a century known as the Age of Reason, or the Enlightenment. Classical values dominated thought and taste in Goethe's youth. This means that the influence of Greek and Roman thought was strongly felt in education and culture. Goethe's early education, therefore, stressed Greek and Roman literature and the predominance of reason over feeling. There was no emphasis in Goethe's family on Christian values—Goethe's father did not consider himself a Christian—although the culture was steeped in religious tradition, and Goethe knew the Bible very well. Goethe's father sent him to the University of Leipzig at sixteen, to study law and absorb the values of the time.

But the young Goethe returned home after two years, suffering from mental strain. It may be that he was beginning to rebel emotionally and intellectually against Classical restraints, for he spent the next year or two in his Frankfurt home investigating some very unclassical ideas. His mother had taken up Pietism, a kind of fundamentalist Christianity that stressed the individual believer's direct contact with God. In addition, Goethe discovered the works of medieval mystics, who were sometimes described as magicians because they believed in a secret knowledge accessible only to those who had been initiated. These studies led Goethe to alchemy, which, in medieval times, had represented a genuine attempt to understand the world scientifically. In Goethe's time, the study of alchemy was in part a means of re-creating the past.

When Goethe returned to university studies, he went to Strasbourg, where he met a young theologian and philosopher named Johann Gottfried von Herder (1744–1803), who was beginning to make a mark in German intellectual circles. Under Herder's influence, Goethe became part of the Sturm und Drang ("storm and stress") literary movement that emphasized naturalistic, individualistic, anti-Classical feeling. (Classicism stresses form, structure, logic, and rational thought.) The Sturm und Drang writers were obsessed with the idea of liberated genius, sure that feelings were more important than intellect, and impressed with the simplicity of folk poetry. They believed in the natural goodness of man, admired William Shakespeare, and saw literature as a means of searching for the Absolute, or that which underlay all of existence. Most intellectual historians see the Sturm und Drang movement as a forerunner of Romanticism (which stressed feeling and nature) in the nineteenth century, but in its search for originality and abstract truth, the Sturm und Drang movement still had much in common with the Enlightenment. Bear in mind, however, that much of Goethe's writing, especially Part I of *Faust*, is usually thought of as Romantic.

In the early 1770s, Goethe wrote a novel in the form of letters, *The Sorrows of Young Werther*, which indulges in emotions to a point you may find difficult to tolerate now. At the end of the story, Werther kills himself because he cannot live with the woman he loves, who's already engaged. *Werther*, together with a play about a German outlaw hero, *Götz von Berlichingen*, brought Goethe fame and established him as one of the leaders of the Sturm and Drang movement.

Almost incidentally, Goethe qualified as a lawyer during these years and practiced in Frankfurt, where he witnessed the tragic case of a young maidservant condemned to death for the murder of her baby. Goethe felt deep compassion for the girl, who suffered from the injustice of a social order that allowed men of the upper class to ruin girls casually. He may have had a pang of guilt himself, because he was something of a ladies' man. Throughout his life, from his teens to his seventies, he either fell passionately in love with women who attracted him physically or worshipped women with whom he felt a platonic (spiritual) affinity. When he finally married, in 1806, he was fifty-seven.

The young maidservant whose life was ruined became Gretchen in Part I of *Faust*. You can understand why he began writing it in the early 1770s, about the same time as his Sturm und Drang works. Faust was a rebel against authority who strove

constantly to know and experience everything. He
had immense courage, which the Sturm and Drang
followers admired, and he was a figure straight out
of German history. Another noted German dramatist, Gotthold Ephraim Lessing (1729–1781), had
called for a play on the Faust theme and had even
composed a scene himself. The addition of the
Gretchen story brought to the work an element of
folk simplicity.

Bot Goethe's *Faust* is no simple updating of the
legend. His hero does not sell his soul to the Devil—
he makes a bet with him, and the Devil, Mephistopheles, loses. Faust does not disobey God's
commands, as he does in the legend. Goethe's God
has complete confidence in Faust's good sense and
gives His permission for Mephistopheles to tempt
Faust in order to keep him on his toes. Goethe
wrote a *Faust* that is definitely not a Christian cautionary tale. What, then, is it? You'll want to keep
the question in mind as you read the work.

In 1775, Goethe's life was swept in another direction and he didn't return to *Faust* for many years.
He was invited to live at the court of the young
duke of Weimar, who wanted Goethe as a central
attraction for the intellectual and artistic life of
Weimar. Goethe was to spend most of the rest of
his life there, writing, becoming involved with the
theater, pursuing private scientific studies, and, as
a favor to his patron, serving as an administrator
for the tiny duchy. Goethe's friend Herder (who
may have been a model for Mephistopheles) set-
tled in Weimar, along with other writers and
thinkers, who, with Goethe, made Weimar an intellectual center for the next half-century or so.

In 1786, Goethe did something surprising. He

left the Weimar court abruptly and journeyed to Italy. He spent much of the next two years in Rome, where he studied the art of the Classical period, completing more than one thousand drawings of Classical statues and buildings. During his journey, about which he later wrote, Goethe immersed himself in the Classical style, but he did not turn away completely from Romanticism. Some of his works display a tension, an uneasy balance between the two styles. A drama such as *Iphigenie in Tauris* (1787) is unmistakably Classical, in theme as well as in form and style, but what about *Faust*? In *Faust*, Part II, a work of his later years, Goethe attempts a union of the Classical and Romantic in the marriage of Faust and Helen of Troy.

Goethe's Classical side gave him a love of order—social, political, as well as personal—that prevented him from admiring the French Revolution, which broke out in 1789, the year after he returned from Italy. While Romantic writers were hailing the new spirit in France, Goethe shuddered at its excesses. Safe and secure at Weimar, he published the first portions of *Faust*, called *Faust: Ein Fragment* ("Faust: A Fragment"), in 1790. He continued to write plays and novels, as well as some of the poetry that has earned him the title of the greatest lyric poet in the German language.

In 1794, Goethe began a friendship, almost a collaboration, with the poet and dramatist Friedrich von Schiller (1759–1805). Goethe invited Schiller to live at Weimar, where they worked together until Schiller's death. Under Schiller's prodding, Goethe took up *Faust* and by 1808 completed what we know as Part I. Goethe, however, realized that what he had to say would require a second part, but he didn't immediately begin Part II. *Faust* languished again, until 1825. Pressure to return to it came this time from Johann Peter Eckermann (1792–1854), who had become Goethe's literary secretary in 1823 and immortalized himself by recording and publishing their talks together on literary and other subjects (*Conversations with Eckermann*, 1836–1848). Goethe wrote Part II of *Faust* between 1825 and 1831. He was then in his late seventies and early eighties.

It's not always easy to see *Faust* as a whole. Part I was the only portion of the drama published in Goethe's lifetime, and it became the basis for a popular opera by the nineteenth-century French Romantic composer, Charles Gounod, so that the general public began to feel that *Faust* consisted essentially of the Faust and Gretchen story and the bet between Faust and the Devil. The complete *Faust* was printed in 1832, as the first volume of Goethe's collected works published after his death. It is recognized as his masterpiece.

You now have the opportunity to take the same journey that Goethe took in composing *Faust*. Don't be afraid to make up your own mind about *Faust*, even if your conclusions differ from what others have thought. It is the mark of a masterpiece like *Faust* that it continues to yield new and exciting meanings as each generation of readers encounters it.

THE PLAY

The Plot

The story of *Faust* begins in Heaven. Mephistopheles, the Devil, is visiting the Lord, complaining, as usual, about the Lord's creation, man. When the Lord asks him whether he knows Faust, Mephistopheles, saying he does, seizes the opportunity to bet with the Lord that he can lead Faust astray. The Lord is quite confident that Faust knows the right way; he's also tolerant of Mephistopheles, whose role is to keep prodding man into action.

Faust is a very learned professor, who, however, is dissatisfied with human knowledge, which by its nature is limited. Using magic, he conjures up the Earth Spirit in his darkened study. Regarding himself as more than mortal, he tries to claim the Earth Spirit as a colleague, but the Spirit rejects him scornfully and disappears. Despairing, Faust contemplates suicide. He is saved by the sound of the bells welcoming Easter morning. He and his research assistant, Wagner, go out into the sunlight and enjoy the greetings of the crowd, which remembers the medical attention given to the people by Faust and his father. Faust is still depressed, denying the value of medicine and feeling torn between the two souls in him, one longing for earthly pleasures, the other seeking the highest spiritual knowledge. A dog follows Faust and Wagner home.

Back in his study, Faust tries to translate the Gospel of St. John, while the dog becomes restless.

Eventually, the animal changes shape so monstrously that Faust realizes he is dealing with the Devil. Presto! There is Mephistopheles!

At this first meeting, Mephistopheles introduces himself and his powers to Faust; then he tricks Faust into sleeping so that he can leave. When he returns, magnificently dressed, Mephistopheles makes a bet with Faust. He agrees to do anything Faust wants, but if Faust ever says that he is totally satisfied, that the moment is so perfect he wants time to stop, then he will die and Mephistopheles will have his soul. They sign their pact in blood.

Mephistopheles tries to please his "master." He takes him to a Witch's Kitchen, where Faust is magically transformed into a young man. When Faust meets Margarete—called Gretchen, the shortened version of her name—walking in the street, he is consumed with passion for her and orders Mephistopheles to arrange for him to possess her immediately.

Mephistopheles, who has more sense than his master about how to conduct love affairs, takes Faust into Gretchen's room while she is absent. They leave a casket of jewels, but Gretchen's mother, when it is found, insists that it be given to the Church. Mephistopheles then leaves a second present of jewelry, which Gretchen this time conceals at a neighbor's house.

From that point Gretchen is doomed. Faust seduces her and makes her pregnant. When Gretchen's brother, Valentine, intervenes, cursing her as a whore, Mephistopheles, with Faust at his side, kills Valentine.

Mephistopheles takes Faust off to a witches' celebration, Walpurgis Night, on top of a mountain, where at first Faust is fascinated by the fantastic whirl of magical apparitions but then is disturbed by reminders of Gretchen. By the time he returns to the real world, Gretchen has been condemned to death for the murder of her illegitimate baby and has gone mad in her prison cell. As Mephistopheles drags Faust away, a heavenly voice calls out that Gretchen's soul is saved.

Part II of *Faust* begins in a natural setting with Faust recovering from his horror. Mephistopheles is preparing to introduce Faust to the great world of politics and power. They appear at the Emperor's court, where Mephistopheles solves economic problems by suggesting that the court issue paper money against the value of gold hidden underground.

Using his magic, Mephistopheles stages for the court a magnificent masque, a pageant of symbolic figures, in which Faust appears dressed as the god of wealth. The Emperor himself arrives, dressed as the Greek god Pan. The entire pageant dissolves in magic fire, which impresses the Emperor so much that he asks for more. He wants to see the famous beauty of Greek mythology, Helen of Troy, and her Trojan lover, Paris.

Mephistopheles tells Faust that such a request will strain their powers, for Faust must go down to seek the help of the Mothers, mysterious beings who control the underworld. Mephistopheles assembles the court to witness Faust's evocation of Paris and Helen, in the form of visions. Faust is so overcome with Helen's beauty, and with the desire to possess her, that he faints as the visions fade.

He is transported back into his study, which he

had left years before and has not revisited since. Wagner, who has become a doctor, is trying to produce human life. Mephistopheles' presence adds the final spark. A tiny man, Homunculus, appears like a bright light in a test tube. Homunculus leads the way to the plains of the Peneios river in Greece, where the Walpurgis Night will take place.

As they meet mythological figures from literature, Faust discovers a way to reach Helen in the underworld. Mephistopheles finds a disguise as one of the Phorcyads (three female monsters who share one eye and one tooth). And Homunculus discovers a way to realize his being by uniting with a sea goddess. He smashes his test tube against the chariot of Galatea (a goddess of beauty) in a blaze of light, symbolizing creation.

Helen has come back from the underworld at the point where she is returning to her original home in Sparta, after spending ten years in Troy. She is frightened of the revenge that her husband, King Menelaus, is planning against her. Mephistopheles, in the shape of Phorcyas, points out that she can be rescued by walking to a medieval castle. There, Faust, dressed as a medieval knight, greets her. They unite to produce a son, Euphorion, who is the spirit of poetry (and a symbol for the English poet, Lord Byron, whose "unsatisfied nature" and striving for a heroic form of existence, as Goethe told Eckermann, epitomized the contemporary Romantic poet).

Euphorion has a brilliant, though short, career but when he tries to fly he crashes to the ground. Helen returns to the underworld, broken by the tragedy that her beauty seems always to bring about. Faust is left only with her garments.

Again, Faust must reconcile himself to being a failure. He plunges into a scheme to reclaim land from the sea and control it. In order to gain the land, he and Mephistopheles must help the Emperor suppress a rebellion. They bring to the battle the Three Mighty Men who fought with King David. They win the battle through magic, but barely.

With Mephistopheles' help, Faust reclaims the land. He builds a magnificent palace overlooking the shore but is irritated because he has allowed an old couple, Baucis and Philemon, to keep their tiny cottage and a chapel on the land. He asks Mephistopheles to remove the couple to a small farm he has promised them. Mephistopheles takes the Three Mighty Men to do the job; they burn down the cottage and the chapel, killing the old couple and a traveler who was visiting them.

Although Faust has failed again, he does not stop striving and planning. He is struck blind by Care, who tries to make him worry about his coming death. He dies reflecting that he has never found any moment so beautiful, so pleasant, that he wanted it to linger. So Mephistopheles loses his bet. The Devil cannot claim Faust's soul, but he tries to snatch it by trickery. He is outmaneuvered, however, by a chorus of angels, who are so sexually alluring that Mephistopheles becomes distracted by their charms and doesn't notice they are stealing away Faust's soul.

Faust's soul is carried to Heaven by the angels and by the souls of children who have died young. The three penitent women of Christianity pray to the Virgin Mary to save Faust's soul. When Gretchen adds her voice to theirs, the Virgin Mary allows her to lead Faust's soul upward. His journey is completed and he is at rest in Heaven.

The Characters

The following is a discussion of the major characters in *Faust*. There are in addition many other interesting, if less developed, characters, and they are discussed at the appropriate places in The Play section of this guide.

Faust

While Faust has clearly recognizable human characteristics, he is larger than life. He embodies the best and the worst in man, and in many ways he is a symbol of all humanity. Faust is involved in most of the scenes, but he probably reveals himself most clearly through his monologues and through his conversations with Mephistopheles. The monologues show a man without satisfaction or inner peace, always striving. He is continually reaching for more knowledge, more power, more experience. He is also changeable, given to despair when he can't get what he wants. His striving leads inevitably to failure. Some readers have seen these failures as Faust's tragedy, for everything he touches turns to dust. But in these failures he represents humanity, for, as the Lord declares in the Prologue in Heaven, man must make mistakes while he strives.

On one important score, Faust comes out ahead. He bets Mephistopheles that he will never find one moment so fulfilling that he will say to it, "Stay, Thou art so fair!" Faust never does. So he frustrates the Devil and justifies the Lord's confidence in him. It is for his striving, his never giving in, that he is finally saved and his soul carried upward.

In Faust's relations with Mephistopheles you see

an arrogant, impatient man, who uses any means available to get what he wants. Faust is absolutely clear about his relationship to Mephistopheles—Mephistopheles is a servant. In his other relations, you see the brilliance of Faust, why he has the genius to represent humanity. He is capable of passionate romantic love, of courageous action, of large-scale organization. He will probably win your sympathy, even in his ill-fated affair with Gretchen. Try to imagine what it must be like to pick up the pieces of your life after you have caused the destruction of a beautiful young girl and three other innocent people (her mother, brother, and baby). Faust does it.

You may admire Faust more than you like him. It's hard to think of relating to him, although you may recognize parts of his character in your own actions and those of people around you. Because he is all of us, he isn't really any one of us.

Mephistopheles

It may seem strange, but some think that Mephistopheles, the Devil, is more human than Faust. Mephistopheles is a cynic, and cuts things down to size with his quick wit. He calls the Lord an "old gent," satirizes the university faculty, teases the mythological creatures he meets on the Peneios River, and ends scenes with comments that puncture inflated sentiments. Several explanations have been given for Mephistopheles' name, including that it derives from the Greek, *Me-phausto-philes*, meaning "No Friend of Faust" and that it comes from the Hebrew *Mephiztophel*, "corrupter and liar."

In *Faust*, Mephistopheles is the spirit of negation, "the spirit that always denies." In that respect, he is the exact opposite of God, who is the spirit of creation. Why did Goethe make Mephistopheles seem so human? Some readers believe that Goethe wanted to suggest that this spirit of negation is within man. Others believe that Goethe didn't think man was simple enough to fall for a stupid devil. Because man has intellect, they argue, the Devil must have intellect. Some even see Mephistopheles as the symbol of intellect without feeling.

Mephistopheles is a servant, both of God and of Faust, and has the soul of a servant, of a person who must obey but resents it and takes every opportunity to assert what domination he can. He is a servant of God because he is a part of Creation; he has to exist in order for good to exist. He is a servant of Faust because God allows it. But he isn't always willing to do what his master wants, especially at critical moments. He messes up orders, often with disastrous effects on innocents like Baucis and Philemon. He thinks he knows better than his master how to woo women and takes over the wooing of Gretchen. At the same time, he exercises his own authority when he can.

You're never quite confident that Mephistopheles can control his trickery and magic. For example, it's not clear whether the Mothers really do exist or are just invented on the spot to cover Mephistopheles' incompetence. During the battle with the rebellious emperor, it looks as if the real Emperor, who has trusted Mephistopheles, is going to lose. He isn't a trustworthy Devil.

But no devil is trustworthy. You'll remember that the Lord has deliberately "paired" him with mankind to keep man on his toes. The Devil's job is to "play the deuce, to stir, and to entice." He's there to keep things off balance, so that man is always reaching for what the Devil seems to offer.

Above all, Mephistopheles loses his bet. As the Lord foretold at the beginning, Faust would know the right way and never be satisfied by anything Mephistopheles could do.

Margarete (Gretchen)

Margarete, or Gretchen (a favorite name in German folk tales), is a more lifelike character than Mephistopheles and Faust; she is a person you would recognize if you met her. She is a sweet, simple, modest girl, who lives at home and helps her mother. She knows right from wrong (as you can see from her polite refusal of Faust's advances at first) and has an innocent religious faith of the kind idealized by Romantic writers.

Her downfall is a puzzle to you only in the sense that all similar cases are puzzles. Why does such a girl give in to presents and flattery? Gretchen's mother is so strict that she gives the first casket of jewels to the Church. Gretchen then responds with deception, storing the second set of jewels in the house of her neighbor, Martha. Perhaps if her mother had been more understanding, or Martha less of a "pimp," or Gretchen morally stronger in herself, the tragedy wouldn't have happened.

Gretchen is up against the Devil, who by definition has no morals and no mercy. He's been told to get her for Faust and he does. From the moment she gives in to Faust, she begins to lose herself. She seeks comfort in her simple religious faith but cannot withstand society's disapproval and her brother's curse. She becomes mad, kills her baby, and is condemned to die.

Gretchen's sad story was based on a court case known to Goethe. He uses her story for social purposes, to make the point that she is a victim of an attractive man of a class higher than her own. Some girls might have been strong enough to resist the temptation or even to put up with the guilt, but they would not have been sufficient for Goethe the dramatist. He needed a fragile girl like Gretchen who trusted in a simple religious faith and her own feelings.

Wagner

Wagner is called Faust's "famulus," a combination of servant and research assistant who lives and studies close to Faust, his mentor. Wagner is the sort of person you feel you ought to admire but can't bear. He has his heart in the right place, and says all the expected things. Look at him trying to appease Faust with praise of his father. You can't object to what he says, but it doesn't reflect Faust's mood at all.

It's appropriate that Wagner can't give the spark of life to Homunculus. He becomes a scientist after working hard and developing his abilities. But it takes the presence of Mephistopheles to produce Homunculus, who immediately shows all the brilliant intuition his "father," Wagner, lacks. Wagner is left alone again, deserted by Homunculus as he was by Faust years earlier, to live the conventional life he is fitted for. Wagner's soul cannot soar. He and his kind do the work of the world.

Student-Baccalaureus

The only character besides Faust, Mephistopheles, and Wagner common to both Parts I and II of *Faust* is the Student whom Mephistopheles interviews in Faust's study and then meets again as a graduate. He begins timid and wide-eyed, eager to learn from Mephistopheles, who is disguised as Faust, and surprised when his mentor talks obscenely about a doctor's female patients.

When you see him again, as Baccalaureus (a graduate), how changed he is! He knows everything, despises his elders, and sounds like a student radical of the 1960s when he says that anyone over thirty is as good as dead. He personifies, as Goethe told his secretary, Eckermann, the arrogance of youth. Mephistopheles backs away from him because he's so obnoxious.

The Emperor

The Emperor is found only in Part II, where he appears in two of the five acts. The character derives from the traditional Faust story, which includes a visit to an Emperor's court, where Faust and Mephistopheles amaze the court with their magic tricks.

Goethe's Emperor is an incompetent, vain ruler who seeks personal pleasure at the expense of his kingdom. The Emperor permits Mephistopheles to trick him into signing an order authorizing the printing of paper money, thus ruining the state economy. Then he allows a rival emperor to collect a rebellious army, and again acts helplessly until Mephistopheles uses magic to defeat them. When you see him for the last time, he is submitting to the blackmail of the Archbishop, while protesting under his breath.

Helen

Helen is not so much a character as an embodied myth, as she herself recognizes. She is the heroine of Homer's *Iliad*, a great Greek epic poem. (When Paris fell in love with her and stole her from her husband King Menelaus of Sparta, the Trojan War was ignited. Helen's former suitors had sworn an oath to defend her husband's rights. They formed an army that defeated the Trojans and reunited Helen with Menelaus.) In *Faust*, she is afraid for her own safety, as well as for that of the chorus. But she is courageous, as you see when she agrees to seek help from the medieval knight, who turns out to be Faust. She shows her queenly graciousness when she forgives Lynceus, the watchman, for not announcing her arrival.

In the end, Helen is defeated by her own beauty. As she says, beauty and good fortune do not mix. You feel her intense emotion as she embraces Faust one last time and follows their son, Euphorion, to the underworld.

Other Elements
FORM AND STRUCTURE

Faust is a verse drama in two parts. Part I has three preliminary sections (Dedication, Prelude in the Theater, and Prologue in Heaven) and twenty-five scenes, each with a name, usually describing the setting. Part II, like many conventional plays, is divided into five acts, and each act contains scenes with descriptive names. The total length of *Faust I* and *II* is 12,110 lines of poetry. It would take some twenty hours for the play to be performed uncut!

Because the play does not have the usual act and scene structure throughout, the lines are numbered consecutively from beginning to end, like those in a poem.

There are three major questions regarding the
structure of *Faust:* Is it one play or two? Is it a play
at all? Is it a tragedy?

Is *Faust* One Play or Two?

You'll want to make up your own mind about the
unity of *Faust.* Some readers argue that the two
parts are separate and should be treated as such.
It's true that the story of Part I is better known
than anything in Part II, perhaps because of Gounod's opera, *Faust,* which is based on Part I.

Other readers believe that the two parts form an
essential unity. The parts are divided artificially,
because they were composed at different times in
Goethe's life. These readers believe that if you separate one part from the other, you'll miss major
themes.

The original Faust story had a fairly simple structure. Faust, or Faustus, as he was originally called—
the Latin word *faustus* means "lucky"—made a
bargain with the Devil and signed it in blood. The
Devil takes Faust to a student tavern—where the
two fool the students with magically produced
wine—and then to the Emperor's court, where Faust
magically calls Helen of Troy from the dead and
falls in love with her. At the end of twenty-four
years, Faust vainly calls on God's mercy as Mephistopheles drags him away to Hell.

Some of the problems in Goethe's *Faust* are caused
by the different structures of the two parts, as well
as by the change in subject matter from Part I to
Part II. Part I has no act divisions and the scenes
are differentiated by names, not scene numbers.
In it, Faust makes a bet with the Devil—the Devil
will be his servant, and he will possess his soul at

death unless Faust is never able to say he is satisfied. The rest of Part I concerns the seduction and
ruin of Gretchen by Faust. In the end, Gretchen is
saved.

The atmosphere of Part I is gloomy. The action
takes place in and around the German university
town where Faust lives, except for the scenes in
the Witch's Kitchen and on the mountain, where
the Walpurgis Night celebrations are held. It is also
unified by the characters' preoccupation with their
relationship to God. Faust explains his religious
faith in his Credo, and attempts to translate the
Gospel of St. John. Mephistopheles has to admit
that he is part of God's scheme, with a duty to stir
up mankind. Gretchen has a conventional, simple
faith that increases the pathos of her suffering.

Part I, therefore, seems basically to consist of
one piece. The impression of unity is even stronger
if you interpret the last few lines to mean that
Mephistopheles is taking Faust away to Hell as
Gretchen is executed. Part I also was a product of
the "Sturm und Drang" phase of Goethe's writing
and is full of emotion, a sign of Romanticism.

Part II has a different structure and much more
varied subject matter. It has the conventional five
acts divided into scenes, but, again, these have
names instead of numbers. In it, Faust serves an
Emperor, marries Helen of Troy, becomes a successful man, and, in the end, gains redemption.
The work for the Emperor and the appearance of
Helen of Troy are from the original Faust story.
But the union of Classical and Romantic, in the
marriage of Faust and Helen and the birth of their
son; the story of Homunculus; the Carnival masque
and the making of paper money at the Emperor's

court; the Classical Walpurgis Night; Faust's land-
reclamation project; the tragedy of Baucis and Philemon; and the salvation of Faust, are Goethe's
own inventions.

Some elements are clearly intended to produce
unity. For example, the two Walpurgis Nights are
balanced against one another. In addition, Gretchen
and Helen are placed in contrast—the simple German maiden and the legendary Greek beauty. The
Prologue has its counterpart in the final scene,
where Faust's soul is carried off to Heaven.

There is no doubt that if you read the two parts
separately you will have a different experience from
what you would have if you read Parts I and II
together. The question is, what kind of unity does
the work have? You may find yourself on the fence,
believing in a weak unity of the two parts but convinced that some sections are more successful than
others.

Is *Faust* a Play?

Faust doesn't have the structure you probably expect in a play—a rising action that reaches a climax, and then a falling action during which the
plot is resolved. It has been called a "cosmic vision
or dream," and readers have thought of it as a
series of episodes in dramatic form—somewhat like
an epic.

An epic is a poem or narrative on the largest
scale, dealing with national origins and heroes (as
do Homer's *Iliad* and *Odyssey* and Virgil's *Aeneid*)
or man's relation to God (as do Dante's *Divine
Comedy* and Milton's *Paradise Lost*). Epics can have
the structure of a journey (for example, the *Odyssey*
is a journey). *Faust* is a journey through the life of

a hero who is meant to symbolize Western man. Its episodic structure reflects the succession of events in Faust's life. Although *Faust* may seem to lack a governing form, certain features give it internal structure. The diagram on page 24 shows a structure that some readers perceive as holding the whole drama together.

Faust begins on the left side in despair. His spirits rise with his love for Gretchen but are dashed when she dies. He moves from the sphere of personal, subjective action to intellectual action as he achieves union with Helen. Again, he loses his love, but this time on a higher level—he is less overwhelmed than he was by Gretchen's death. Finally, his immortal part is taken to Heaven in a mystical ceremony of salvation.

Notice that the diagram indicates no connection between Faust and Heaven at the beginning: Faust attains Heaven through the jagged upward progress of his life. You will realize, as you read the drama, that it isn't quite as neat as this diagram suggests. The intellectual and political actions overlap, and Faust's enjoyment of his reclaimed land occupies only a part of Act V. But the diagram will help guide you in the unfamiliar territory of Goethe's creation.

Is *Faust* a Tragedy?

Goethe subtitled *Faust* "A Tragedy," thereby presenting his readers with a puzzle. In what sense is *Faust* a tragedy? To the Greeks, who developed the literary form called tragedy, as well as to the Elizabethans (Shakespeare and his contemporaries), tragedy meant a play dealing with the fall of

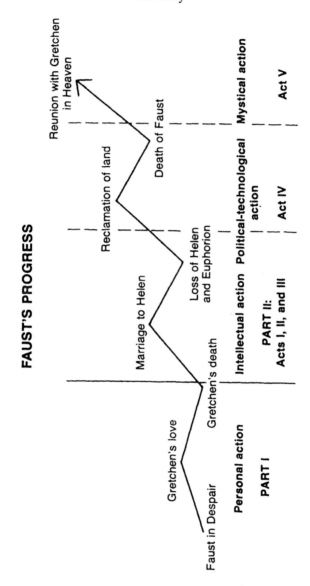

FAUST'S PROGRESS

Faust in Despair

Gretchen's love

Gretchen's death

Marriage to Helen

Loss of Helen
and Euphorion

Reclamation of land

Death of Faust

Reunion with Gretchen
in Heaven

Personal action	Intellectual action	Political-technological action	Mystical action
PART I	PART II: Acts I, II, and III	Act IV	Act V

a great man as a result of a fatal flaw in his character. But Faust is saved at the end.

Since Faust represents mankind, is Goethe saying that man's life is tragic because man must always strive and err without satisfaction? If so, why is Faust carried off to Heaven at the end? Perhaps Goethe merely meant by "tragedy" a drama of serious and lofty subject because he wanted *Faust* to be treated as the highest form of art. Tragedy, like epic, has traditionally been regarded as the most demanding form for both writer and audience, dealing with the deepest philosophical and moral questions.

SETTING

If you're asked where the action of *Faust* takes place, you're justified in answering "Everywhere!" The action takes place in Heaven; in Germany and the Greek Islands; in the air above the earth; in mountains, forests, caves, rivers and river valleys, and the sea. Its settings are those required by the story as it moves, episode by episode, through the epic tale of Faust's life.

As with space, so also with time. Faust is a Renaissance scholar, and the first few scenes retain a rough sense of that historical period. But the Walpurgis Night is timeless, especially in its relationship to Gretchen's story. The Emperor's court seems roughly contemporary with Goethe's time, for the introduction of paper money is discussed. But with Faust's journey down to the Mothers and the subsequent raising of the ghosts of Helen and Paris, things become hazy.

Time has no meaning in the Helen act, where

Faust, who belongs in the sixteenth century, becomes a medieval knight from a period three hundred years earlier in order to meet a mythological queen from the times of classical Greek literature. Between them they produce a son, who resembles the poet Byron, Goethe's contemporary—all without any break in the action!

After this, nothing surprises the reader, not even the onstage transporting of Faust's soul to Heaven. The final scene has no possible historical time, for it combines the fathers of the Church, biblical characters, and Gretchen from Part I.

Goethe felt free to place the story of Faust's life in such a vast setting because Faust represents all mankind. He has all the vices and virtues of mankind on a grand scale. He is supposed to be larger than life and you need to see him in a setting of cosmic scale. He is constantly striving to reach beyond the limits of the physical world and humanity, constantly striving for understanding and fulfillment—and he never gives up.

THEMES

Faust has a general overarching theme—man's life on earth and quest for knowledge and power. Naturally, such an ambitious theme must include many subthemes. Some of these are listed below, and you will be able to add to the list as you read the play.

1. CONSTANT STRIVING

The stories on which *Faust* is based were cautionary tales for Christians: Man must not seek to go beyond the limits set by God. In those stories,

the Devil promises Faust unlimited power for a
limited time and then, as repayment, takes Faust's
soul to Hell.

Goethe's *Faust* does not contain such a bargain
with the Devil. Instead, it has two wagers. The
Lord bets Mephistopheles that he won't be able to
make Faust deviate from "the appointed course,"
and Faust bets Mephistopheles that he won't be
able to make any moment so pleasurable that Faust
will cry out for time to stop. Thus, the bet between
Faust and Mephistopheles concerns fulfillment. If
Faust is ever tempted to stop reaching for something new, he will forfeit his soul. But he doesn't
lose it, because he is never satisfied, emotionally,
spiritually, or intellectually.

You may have heard the expression "the Faustian spirit." It refers to the restless striving for
knowledge and power. The Faustian spirit cannot
stop. It is human to strive ever upward and, un-
fortunately, often to make mistakes in the process.
The striving theme raises an important question:
Does human striving inevitably lead to destruction
and self-destruction, or is there some other human
quality to balance these effects?

2. CLASSICAL VS. ROMANTIC SPIRITS
In Western thought since the eighteenth century
there's been a conflict between the Classical and
the Romantic. Romantic means what is emotional,
subjective, spontaneous, springing from the common people, like Gretchen. Faust's relationship with
her is intense but destructive, for both of them give
way to uncontrolled emotions. The atmosphere of
Faust Part I reflects the mood of Romanticism. The
Classical spirit is associated with the aristocracy of

Helen, traditional formality like that of Greek tragedy, restraint, and the subordination of the individual to the collective good.

The marriage of Faust, representing Romanticism typical of Germany and Northern Europe, and
Helen, representing Classicism typical of Greece
and Southern Europe, shows the tension between
the two sides. The marriage can take place only in
the imagination, and its products are short-lived,
like the poet Euphorion.

Like the Faustian theme, the tension between
the "Classical" and the "Romantic" spirits is a constant feature of our lives. A vivid example was the
1960s student movement, which in the name of
individual freedom questioned social authority and
restraint.

3. "WOMAN ETERNAL/DRAWS US ON HIGH"

Goethe believed that the guiding force of the
universe is love, and he knew that throughout
Western cultural history, woman has been the most
tangible, understandable symbol of love. Think,
for example, of the centrality of the "earth mother"
or "mother goddess" to ancient cult religions. Or
of the importance of the Virgin Mary to Christianity. And don't forget that Dante, in his *Divine
Comedy*, is admitted into Paradise by his model of
pure love, Beatrice. In *Faust*, Helen of Troy is the
symbol of pure love and beauty, while Gretchen
is actually Faust's savior. Even the mysterious, pri-
mal forces of the earth are called the Earth *Mothers*.
Woman Eternal, then, seems to be the symbol of
divine love and forgiveness and of the principle of
creation. The symbol of Woman Eternal trium-

phantly leads man not to strive for the world beyond its reach, but toward creation, beauty, joy,
and love.

4. LIFE IS SIMULTANEOUSLY COMIC AND TRAGIC

You may often wonder why Goethe called *Faust*
a tragedy. Much of it is hilariously funny, especially when Mephistopheles is around, but also in
the interludes like the Walpurgis Night's Dream
and the carnival masque at the Emperor's court.
Wagner and the Student/Baccalaureus are clearly
figures of fun. Homunculus's wit sparkles like the
light he sends out from his test tube. The comic
spirit is an essential part of life and therefore of
Faust. By making so much of *Faust* comic, Goethe
is making a statement about his picture of human
life. It is not tragic exclusively, any more than it is
Romantic exclusively. It is comic even while it is
tragic.

5. PEACE AND SALVATION ARE FOUND IN THE NATURAL WORLD

Faust expresses a mystical connection between
humans and the natural world. The Earth Spirit is
Faust's ideal. Some readers believe that Mephistopheles was sent by the Earth Spirit, so that he
is an essential element of the natural world. Look
at the settings of Faust's monologues in Part II—a
landscape, a mountain top. Faust is carried up to
heaven over mountain gorges. The Classical Walpurgis Night, with its earthquakes, meteor, and
procession across the Aegean Sea, is a celebration
of nature as the origin of human life and its con-
tinual refreshment.

6. "GOD'S SOVEREIGN WORKS STILL TOWER"

Although *Faust* does not convey a traditional Christian message, it does express Goethe's view of God's place in the universe. The Lord is a thoroughly tolerant "old gent," in Mephistopheles' words, who has set man in the right direction and knows he can't be lured from it. In this universe, the Devil is part of the scheme. He has an essential role—he keeps man from getting too "lax and mellow." This theology is directly opposed to the Christian view, which sees the Devil as a force dedicated to destroying God's good works.

Because God is infinitely tolerant, man is saved so long as he strives. Gretchen is saved by God (it is a voice from above that cries "Redeemed!"), no matter how much she is condemned by her peers and by the law. Mephistopheles cannot touch her, just as he can't touch Faust's soul. He will always lose, but he will always keep on trying. That is the Devil's job. It is also important to remember here that, unlike in the traditional Faust legend, Goethe's Faust is saved.

STYLE

The great variety of styles in *Faust* reflects the range of the poem's characters and settings. Some readers have said that *Faust* contains more poetic meters (measured, patterned arrangement of syllables) and forms than any other single work. Others think that it is stylistically too exuberant, that its large number of styles sometimes interferes with communicating a clear message.

The styles include a sixteenth-century German form called *Knüttelvers* or *Knittelvers* (doggerel),

which is irregular, though rhymed; ballads and
songs, often as simple as folk songs; the trimeter
(a line of verse with three measured feet) of classical tragedy, as well as the strophes (stanzas of
the chorus as it moves to the right or the left of
the stage) of the choruses; Shakespeare's blank
verse; the Alexandrines (iambic line of twelve syllables) used by the seventeenth-century French
playwright Jean-Baptiste Racine; and prose (for one
memorable scene). Gretchen expresses her feelings in a series of ballads and lyrics, which convey
the folk simplicity of her character.

Faust contains numerous references to the Bible
and ancient literature. It may be difficult for you
as a modern student to follow these allusions, since
the Bible and Greek and Roman literature no longer
occupy the central place in school that they occu-
pied in Goethe's time. Nevertheless, you may find
yourself amazed at how modern a play *Faust* is.
Respond to it as you would to a new work by a
contemporary playwright—for, in spirit, Goethe is
one of us.

The translation of *Faust* used for this Study Guide
is by Walter Arndt (New York: W.W. Norton, 1976).
It was chosen because it tries to faithfully repro-
duce the different rhythms and verse forms of the
original. Of course, a translation that tries to re-
produce the original poetry must lead to compro-
mises, because a translator must at times use words
with slightly different meaning than the original.
Also, expressions used to fit a meter may sometimes seem artificial and strange. Some readers,
indeed, think that a verse translation is simply too
difficult to do well, and they prefer a prose translation that conveys the meaning accurately.

If you do not read German, the best way for you

to get close to the meaning is to compare several translations. There are some fifty translations of *Faust* in English, the vast majority of them translations of Part I alone. Comparing three or four of them is time-consuming, so you shouldn't do it with every line; but some crucial lines need the perspective of at least two or more versions. All translation is also to some degree interpretation, because the word chosen in English is rarely exactly equivalent to the German. The choice of a word is influenced by the translator's view of the poet's meaning.

To give you an idea of the variation in translations, here are versions by four translators of the Lord's important words in the Prologue in Heaven.

> *Walter Arndt:* Man ever errs the while
>   he strives.
> *Philip Wayne:* For man must strive,
>   and striving he must err.
> *Carlyle F. MacIntyre:* Man is doomed to err as
>   long as he strives.
> *Randall Jarrell:* A man must make
>   mistakes, as long as he
>   keeps trying.

The differences between one English translation and another can be more a matter of style than of meaning. The feeling of one translation may be very different from another. Take, for example, lines 338–39:

> Of all the spirits of negation
> The rogue has been least onerous to my mind.
> > *(Arndt)*

> Of all the spirits of negation
> The rogue is least of burdens to be borne.
> > *(Wayne)*

Of all the spirits of denial
The joker is the last that I eschew.
                              (Louis MacNeice)

Of all the spirits that deny
The mischief-maker weighs upon me least.
                                    (Jarrell)

All the translators refer to Mephistopheles as the spirit of negation or denial, and the basic meaning of the passage is the same in each translation, but the images of the Devil as a "rogue" and as a "joker" are very different. Your image of Mephistopheles as a "rogue" or as a "joker" can influence your interpretations of the play.

Because translations differ from the original you should be careful not to attribute to Goethe what may, in fact, be the translator's interpretation. Similarly, be careful not to overemphasize a few words or phrases as you interpret *Faust*, because you may be dealing more with the translator than with Goethe. The larger patterns of the drama, rather than the small details of language, will most likely give you a better idea of the original German text.

SOURCES

The Faust legends stem from the life of a real Faust—Johannes Faustus, a German student of dubious reputation who lived from 1480 to 1540. Some of his contemporaries spoke of him as a faker, or medieval con man, who lived by his wits. Others, however, thought him a magician in league with evil spirits. He was reputed to travel about with a little dog that was really a devil.

Soon after his death, the real Dr. Faustus dis-

appeared into the realm of legend. He became the
scholar who sold his soul to the Devil in exchange
for universal knowledge and magical power. Mar-
tin Luther, the leader of the Protestant Reforma-
tion, was, for example, one of those who believed
Faustus had been in league with the Devil. The
story was popular for its Christian moral: Faustus
was damned for pursuing worldly knowledge instead of studying the Scriptures.

By 1587 a *Faustbuch* (Faust Book) had appeared,
a collection of the various tales being told about
the wicked magician. The book was enormously
popular, both in Germany and elsewhere. Later,
Faust became a popular character in puppet shows
filled with slapstick comedy. But, despite the comedy, the Faust plays always ended with Faust being
dragged off by the Devil, damned because he sought
forbidden knowledge. In addition, numerous
handbooks of magic appeared, bearing Faust's
name. Of course, they always had instructions on
how to avoid the pact with the Devil.

The German poet Gotthold Ephraim Lessing
(1729–1781) was the first to make Faust a hero who
was saved rather than damned. The redemption
was completed by Goethe, in whose great work
Faust represents the virtue of human aspiration.
In Goethe's play, the longing for knowledge that
had once led to Faust's damnation leads to Faust's
salvation.

Goethe probably saw Faust puppet plays during
his childhood and may have produced one of his
own in a puppet theater that his grandmother had
given him. Faust plays were a popular folk entertainment. They were not high art, not the kinds of
plays to be found in court theaters. They owed
their popularity to hell-fire scenes and magic tricks

performed by the devils. The literary source—that is, written text—for these Faust plays was *The History of Dr. Johann Faustus*, published in Frankfurt in 1587, but it is unlikely that Goethe was familiar with it. He probably did know Christopher Marlowe's play, *The Tragical History of Doctor Faustus*, written about 1590, in which Dr. Faustus is dragged off to Hell.

In these stories, Faust is a learned scholar who uses the arts of black magic to raise the Devil. He makes a bargain with the Devil, signing his name in his own blood. The Devil will have Faust's soul after a certain number of years, but during those years the Devil will do whatever Faust commands. The story was a moral tale for Christians, for it warned them against trying to have more than earthly power. In its frightening climax, it depicted Faust being dragged into the fiery mouth of Hell. Yet the story was also a great audience pleaser, because it offered opportunities for magic tricks at the expense of authority figures like the Emperor.

The Gretchen story, which Goethe added from his own experience, is not part of the original Faust plays. But the Helen story does appear in the Faust legend. In some versions, Dr. Faustus raises the spirit of Helen and lives with her for twenty years. The Emperor, too, is part of the original story. Almost everything else comes from Goethe's extensive reading. The figures of the Walpurgis Night come from his study of alchemy, witchcraft, and magic. Those in the Classical Walpurgis Night come from Greek and Roman literature, as do Baucis and Philemon. The Three Mighty Men are found in the Old Testament, and the figures that conduct Faust's soul upward are from Christian tradition.

Goethe derived not only his characters but also

his style from his reading. You will find echoes of
Shakespeare (the character Ariel is borrowed from
The Tempest), Dante, and Byron, as well as a direct
imitation of the Greek playwright Euripides.

The Play

PART I

Part I of *Faust* is divided into twenty-five scenes.
The scenes have descriptive names, not numbers.
Most scenes are short. Line breaks are used in this
guide where scenes are long enough to be treated
in parts. The first three scenes stand outside the
main drama. The most important of them for the
meaning of *Faust* is the Prologue in Heaven.

DEDICATION

Goethe worked on *Faust* intermittently throughout his long life, sometimes setting it aside for a
number of years. The poem that constitutes the
Dedication was written after Goethe had left *Faust*
virtually untouched for more than twenty years,
from 1775 to 1797. The Dedication reflects his mood
as he speaks to the ideas, people, and emotions
connected with the earlier manuscript. He is reminded of lovers and friends, most now dead, who
had read the earlier version of *Faust*. These memo-
ries fill him with emotion and seem to make the
present fade away.

NOTE: *Faust* contains numerous poetic rhythms,
or meters. If you don't understand German, it's

difficult to appreciate the meters and the contribution they make to the play's effect. A translation that follows the original German meters, with their different line lengths and rhyme schemes, will give you some idea of Goethe's poetic genius. The Dedication is written in what is called ottava rima, because it has eight lines, the first six rhyming *ababab* and the last two rhyming with each other, *cc*.

PRELUDE IN THE THEATER

There's an important message in this Prelude that you shouldn't miss. No matter how fanciful *Faust* may seem (its characters include animals, spirits, angels, witches, and God himself, while its settings include mountain tops, palaces, and Greek islands), and even though it is written as poetry, it is a play and Goethe intended it for the theater.

The three characters of the Prelude have three different views as to what makes a good play. The Director, who wants a commercial success, considers what the audience will pay for and what they want in the theater. He calls for plot, action, variety, and spectacle.

In the Poet's remarks, you can see the Romantic theory of poetry. Poetry is the highest essence of things, he says, since it is concerned not with ordinary affairs, but with the most deeply felt emotions and the highest, most abstract principles which make the play meaningful for people in all times and places.

The Merry Person (called Comic Actor or Comedian in some translations) laughs at the Poet's argument. Don't worry about eternal values and

posterity, he says. The successful playwright draws
from real life and makes people laugh.

The Director cuts the debate short by calling for
action. You can imagine him gesturing to include
the whole stage as he promises that the entire universe, including Heaven and Hell, will be presented on his stage.

PROLOGUE IN HEAVEN

As if to prove that the Director isn't exaggerat-
ing, the next scene takes place in Heaven. God is
enjoying the songs of his archangels who praise
the wonders of His creation. You may be surprised
to find Mephistopheles, the Devil, in Heaven as
well, but remember that in Christian theology he
is a "fallen angel." He is a cynic who shifts the
conversation from the praises of God to a criticism
of humanity. Men are unhappy, he says, because
God has given them intelligence and reason. He
compares them to grasshoppers that constantly
jump about and stick their noses into everything.

Abruptly, God asks whether Mephistopheles
knows Faust. Mephistopheles does know him and
thinks he's a strange man who's never satisfied.
Mephistopheles asserts that Faust could easily be
turned away from God. God is tolerant of Faust's
confusion, saying "Man ever errs the while he
strives." In other words, so long as man continues
to search after truth, he will probably make mistakes. Mephistopheles wagers that he can corrupt
Faust, and God says that as long as Faust lives,
Mephistopheles may try to corrupt him. Both are
confident of winning the wager. God even *encour-
ages* Mephistopheles to corrupt Faust.

After God and the angels have disappeared,

Mephistopheles addresses the audience. You already know that he is a cynic and that there is probably a mocking tone in his voice when he refers to God as the "old gent" and comments on what a compliment it is for "a swell [an important person] like him [to be] so man-to-man with the Devil!"

NOTE: All the Faust stories tell of a bet between Faust and the Devil, but only Goethe's *Faust* includes a wager between God and the Devil. Does this scene remind you of the wager between God and Satan in the Old Testament Book of Job? In both Job and *Faust*, God, the creator, allows the Devil, the negator, to try to corrupt an "upright man." The Satan of the Old Testament tries to lure Job away from God by destroying his health and possessions, but you will see that Goethe's Mephistopheles will try to ruin Faust by putting pleasure in his reach. You might also contrast Goethe's Faust, who constantly searches and strives for understanding, with Job, who blindly accepts his fate. In fact, Goethe introduces you in the Prologue to the idea that man must be constantly *striving*. It is this striving toward absolute truth and satisfaction that leads man toward his highest development. The most dangerous sin is inaction, or accepting any condition of life as satisfactory.

You will notice that Goethe uses a great deal of Christian symbolism, and many wonder about his religious attitudes. His religious philosophy is not traditionally Christian, but has been called "religious paganism," meaning that he has religious feelings but doesn't accept any specific beliefs.

NIGHT

Lines 354–520
This is your first view of Faust, in his dark and gloomy study. You'll recognize the Romantic atmosphere right away. Faust is wearing the black gown and square hat of the late medieval scholar.

NOTE: Although Faust is portrayed as a medieval scholar, he is voicing the preoccupations of the late eighteenth century. Toward the end of the century, a new movement, called Romanticism, opposed the rationality of the earlier generation, called the Age of Reason. The Romantics admired intensity of feeling and individual insight. They recognized that not all knowledge was based on logical inquiry. For them, the occult (which focused on casting spells, conjuring spirits, studying astrology, interpreting symbols in magic books, reading signs into natural events, and even taking drugs to induce hallucinations) represented sources of knowledge scorned by Classical thinkers.

The original Faust story, published in 1587, established the tradition that Faust was a teacher in a fifteenth- or sixteenth-century university. He begins this way in Goethe's tragedy, but time and place soon become unclear.

Faust is not satisfied with what his learning has brought him. He feels that he knows nothing and that teaching others is impossible. He wants to know what is not taught in books, to experience direct communion with the spirits of nature.

NOTE: This monologue is the first in a series of speeches by Faust alone on the stage. Each of the speeches marks a different stage in Faust's understanding of his experiences. You should keep track of Faust's monologues so that you can trace his intellectual and emotional development. This scene in his study is a touchstone against which you can measure the later monologues, such as the speech addressed to the Earth Spirit in Forest and Cave in Part I or the monologue in Pleasing Landscape, Part II, Act I.

Opening a book written by a magician of the Middle Ages, Faust first ponders a design representing the Universe, or Macrocosm, and then finds the symbol of the Earth Spirit. This spirit is largely Goethe's own invention and what it means is largely for you to decide. Some readers think that the Earth Spirit is the "guardian spirit" of life which actively lives within nature. Faust brings the Earth Spirit to life, apparently by pronouncing a magic spell, but then he fails miserably to impress the Spirit as an equal.

Does this mean that the Earth Spirit doesn't want to deal with man, only with other spirits? Or does the Spirit think Faust is a companion worthy only for Mephistopheles, not for purer and more powerful spirits? The conversation between Faust and the Spirit is crucial. Faust exclaims that he feels close to the "spirit of deeds," but the Spirit scornfully rejects him, saying that while he may be close to the Spirit, he does not understand it.

The rejection will have serious consequences, but

for the moment Faust is distracted. Wagner, his research assistant, interrupts the scene.

Lines 521–601

You'll recognize Wagner right away as the earnest student who works hard but never really gets the point. He and Faust talk past one another because Wagner insists on asking how to make effective speeches, while Faust is telling him that deep feeling alone is necessary and sufficient.

Wagner is finally persuaded to go back to bed. He asks Faust, however, to continue the discussion tomorrow, Easter Day. Wagner's last line is typical of people like him: "Though I know much, I would know everything."

Lines 602–807

As Faust acknowledges, Wagner took his mind off his bitter disappointment at the Earth Spirit's rejection. In fact, you might see the two scenes as parallel. The Earth Spirit treated Faust much as Faust, on a lower level, treated Wagner.

But now Faust has to face his despair. He is not a spirit but a man subject to emotions and death. As he becomes more and more upset, Faust looks for help in his books, his scientific instruments, and the manuscript he was studying. Looking around the room, he notices a small bottle of poison, which seems the answer to his restlessness. He takes down a beautiful cup that had been used for ceremonial feasts in Faust's family, fills it with the poison, and is about to drink it when the sound of bells bursts in from outside.

In some Christian churches, Easter is celebrated with a daybreak service, so that the rising of Christ from the dead is symbolized by the rising sun. This service has just begun, and its joyful choruses intervene in time to stop Faust from committing suicide.

You can imagine an antiphonal setting (one in which groups or individuals call and respond to one another) between Faust and the choruses. As they sing of the resurrection of Christ, Faust puts his cup of poison down and expresses his feelings about Easter. It's not so much that he responds to the religious meaning of the songs, but that the music reminds him of his youth. On this Easter morning, Faust is saved from death.

NOTE: The Easter service is an example of Goethe's use of Christian symbols for his own purposes. Easter is a ceremony of rebirth, just what is needed to bring Faust back from despair. The choruses of angels, women, and disciples all express Christian promises of consolation and redemption through Christ's resurrection, but they are only symbols of spiritual renewal, not expressions of Goethe's faith.

OUTSIDE THE CITY GATE

Imagine this as a scene in a movie, with the camera isolating groups of people in a large bustling crowd. As Faust moves to the foreground, the camera illustrates his speech, especially its effect on the crowds of brightly dressed people. Clearly, Faust is a new man, speaking from the heart when he exults with the crowd: "Here I am Man, am free to be!"

The peasants revere Faust because he and his father, a physician, had helped them during the plague. Faust says, however, that he and his father don't deserve much praise because their potions caused death as well as cured illness. Here is an early reference to the main theme, that the search for knowledge can cause destruction. Faust is very much aware of his limitations.

His reference to the deaths caused by his potions reminds Faust of his feelings of futility. He tells Wagner that he feels a division within himself. He is pulled toward the world of action and his fellow man, and at the same time toward the ideals that go beyond time and place. He wants a magic cape that will transport him beyond his physical limitations.

___

NOTE: Conflict between two equally balanced sets of values is part of human life. As Faust expresses it here, the conflict is between the world of action and the world of thought. Faust wrestles with himself throughout the play as part of his endless striving. You can see the conflict in the contrast between, on the one hand, Wagner's learning for the sake of learning and, on the other, Faust's admiration for the "deed" and rejection of the people's simple faith in favor of the truth. Do you feel the same conflict in your life? Do you feel there are two forces at war in your mind? How do you resolve them?

You'll remember that Mephistopheles described these two driving forces in lines 304–05 of the Prologue. You won't be surprised that Mephistopheles first appears to Faust shortly after Faust makes

his "two souls" speech. Faust seems to be ready
for Mephistopheles.

Just as Faust expresses his wish for escape into
a free life, he sees a black poodle. Faust senses
that there's something strange about this dog, which
follows him home.

STUDY

In his study, Faust decides to translate the Gospel of St. John into German. He has difficulties
with the first sentence, "In the beginning was the
Word." Faust doesn't think of the Word as the
origin of things. Words are merely a means of expressing essence, and for Faust, essence is action,
the Deed. His reasoning has led him back to the
Old Testament idea of "In the beginning God
created the world." Creation is action, the ruling
force of the universe.

The poodle is restless and growls while Faust
translates the Bible. Faust is about to put him out
when the dog suddenly changes shape and becomes a threatening monster. As other spirits cry
outside, Faust casts spells on the monster. Nothing works until Faust brings out the sign of the
Trinity. At this, a cloud of vapor obscures the
monster, and Mephistopheles appears, dressed as
a traveling scholar.

NOTE: It is important that Faust is not just a
passive bystander in Mephistopheles' efforts to
claim him. The Devil didn't reveal himself to Faust,

but Faust recognized him and conjured him up. Is
it significant that Mephistopheles appears to Faust
as a traveling scholar? Does this disguise make Faust
feel comfortable with him?

Although Mephistopheles doesn't reveal his
identity, he refers to himself as part of a force made
up of both good and evil. Faust, who imagines
things as wholes, has trouble thinking of any being
as only part of a greater scheme of things.

After their talk, Faust discovers that Mephistopheles can't leave because of the magic sign by
the door. Mephistopheles' respect for rules gives
Faust the idea that he may be able to make a bargain with him. Faust becomes more and more ex-
cited because he has the Devil in his power, but
Mephistopheles is anxious to leave. Finally, Mephistopheles calls up a choir of spirits who sing Faust
to sleep while some mice help the Devil escape.

NOTE: Some readers observe that Faust's belief
that Mephistopheles' appearance was only a dream
means that the Devil represents hidden parts of
Faust's nature. (The Romantics believed that the
hidden or "other" side of man's nature was re-
vealed in dreams.) If Faust's nature represents man's
nature, then the Devil must represent hidden parts
of all of us. What do you think?

STUDY

Lines 1529–1850
When Mephistopheles returns, ready to take Faust
out on the town, he finds that Faust's mood has

changed. His negative mood of frustration has returned. He talks of death, and Mephistopheles has to remind him that he didn't commit suicide when he had the chance. Faust's complaints merge in a horrifying curse on all human motivations, from thought through fame and riches to patience itself.

The terrifying moment is intensified by mysterious voices of unseen spirits that first mourn for "beauty destroyed" and then urge renewal. Mephistopheles seizes his chance. He recognizes that a man in the depths of despair is ready for a bet with the Devil. He offers to become Faust's faithful servant and, when Faust wants to know what the Devil will get if he wins, Mephistopheles says that he wants "equal worth" after Faust's death. Presumably, he means that Faust will be his servant in Hell.

Faust makes the famous wager with the Devil that will allow Mephistopheles to collect his soul if Faust loses. Faust, however, makes one crucial change in the wording of the bet. If Mephistopheles ever makes anything so pleasant that Faust cries out with desire to have time stop so that he may enjoy it, then Faust will lose the wager and die at that moment.

NOTE: The idea of a totally fulfilled moment is central to *Faust*. Remember that when the Lord makes his wager with Mephistopheles, he says that man will always make mistakes while he strives. God also says that man must strive continually, and that a Devil like Mephistopheles functions to keep man moving. Mephistopheles' advantage lies in providing life's best experiences for Faust, so Faust may be tempted to call for time to stop and

thereby lose to Mephistopheles. You might want
to draw up a list of the experiences Mephistopheles provides and consider whether he left any out
that might have satisfied Faust.

Faust and Mephistopheles sign the pact in blood.
Faust is anxious to experience all of life, to fulfill
all of human potential, at which point he would
be like God. Mephistopheles has to use persistent
argument and exercise patience to get Faust away
from his identification with "mankind's loftiest
plane," which is unattainable, and down to human pleasures, which are available.

At that moment one of Faust's students knocks
on the door. Since Faust is in no mood for students, Mephistopheles offers to play his part.

Lines 1851–2072
The scene between the unsuspecting student and
Mephistopheles pokes fun at university study and
scholarship in general. Mephistopheles says that
logicians and philosophers attempt to analyze and
pin down thinking but don't understand its intui-
tive components and, therefore, produce students
who can't think at all. The student shows signs of
understanding the importance of the concept, but
Mephistopheles smothers his objection in a stream
of words about words. Mephistopheles then signs
the student's book with the words "You will be
like a god, and come to know good and evil." The
Devil believes that man tries too hard to understand all of life, to be like God. And that is what
makes man unhappy. Mephistopheles thinks man
would be better off concentrating on physical

pleasure. (Remember this scene with the student. He returns in Part II, and you'll be surprised at his development—or not surprised, depending on your view of academic institutions.)

Mephistopheles and Faust now prepare to leave on their first venture together into the world outside Faust's study. When Mephistopheles says, "The small world, then the great we shall peruse," he is forecasting the shape of the drama. In the rest of Part I, Faust explores personal relationships, the small world. Then, in Part II, he moves into politics and technology, as well as an expedition to the time of the Trojan War.

AUERBACH'S TAVERN IN LEIPZIG

A group of students are drinking in a tavern, singing bits of traditional songs. Mephistopheles magically produces wine by drilling holes in the table. Finally, he sets them quarreling with each other and disappears with Faust, who is disgusted by the whole episode.

You may wonder why this scene is here. Some elements of *Faust* belong to the original legend. Among them are Faust's dabbling in the occult, the pact with the Devil written in blood, scenes with Wagner, the Emperor's court, the resurrection of Helen of Troy, and Mephistopheles ' magic tricks with gullible students or courtiers. Thus, a scene where Mephistopheles reveals his powers is traditional. Furthermore, Auerbach's Tavern was a real place that had long been associated with the Faust legend, and its walls were decorated with paintings representing Faust's adventures.

WITCH'S KITCHEN

Mephistopheles takes Faust to a Witch's Kitchen complete with boiling cauldrons and long-tailed monkeys. There, Mephistopheles gives Faust a potion that makes him look and feel much younger. As Faust walks around the kitchen, he comes upon a magic mirror and finds himself fascinated by it. In the mirror he sees the image of the loveliest woman he can imagine. At a distance the image is clear, but it becomes misty and remote when Faust approaches. By the end of this scene, the Devil has prepared Faust for the love affair that will dominate the rest of Part I.

This is the first appearance of an important theme, the beauty and love of women and their influence on men. For Goethe, women represent an ideal that brings out the best in men. Sexual love is therefore a symbol of union, and the vision in the mirror represents the Feminine as an abstraction. You will see how that abstraction is embodied in the two women Faust falls in love with—Gretchen in Part I and Helen of Troy in Part II.

Why does Mephistopheles make Faust thirty years younger? Is it only to make Faust more attractive and energetic and thus to make the rest of Part I believable? Or do you agree with readers who believe that Goethe makes Faust younger so that you may see how he evolves from a young man preoccupied with lust to a mature man who gains insight and understanding?

STREET

As Mephistopheles has predicted, every woman looks like Helen of Troy to Faust, especially the woman Faust meets on the street. This is Margarete, usually called Gretchen, the German diminutive of her name. With great dignity, Gretchen refuses to be picked up by Faust.

NOTE: Most of the last half of Part I is concerned with the sad tale of Gretchen's seduction by Faust and her descent into madness after murdering her baby. This is possibly the most widely known part of *Faust* and some readers think it is the most effective. But don't judge it too quickly. The story of Gretchen falls into place and takes on a different meaning when it is read in the context of the whole play. Here, Faust strives—and fails—on a personal level, but it is not the whole story.

The story of Gretchen is usually called a tragedy. But whose tragedy is it? Is it Gretchen's alone? Or is it Faust's tragedy too? And what causes the tragedy—character, situation, or Mephistopheles' meddling? Keep these questions in mind as you read it.

The contrast between Faust's behavior in the scene in the Witch's Kitchen and this scene on the street is astounding. There, he was entranced by an idea of feminine beauty. Here, he is impatient to get into the girl's bed. He orders Mephistopheles to act, in effect, as his pimp.

What do you think of Faust's passion? Is it understandable in a scholar who has just been made young and introduced to the real world? Or does it represent a universal male attitude toward women? There is no hint here of marriage. Faust's feelings are intense, but they have one object only. Can they be condoned?

A CLEAN LITTLE ROOM

In this very dramatic scene, your sympathy and admiration for Gretchen deepen. She's an innocent young woman, no match for an upper-class suitor aided by a Devil who leaves caskets of jewels in her closet. The cleanliness of her room mirrors the cleanliness of her soul and contrasts with Mephistopheles' lewdness.

Faust's fantasies while sitting in her chair and looking at her bed show that he is in love with his own idea of sexual happiness rather than with a real person. His feelings are deeply stirred, but his conscience is not very active. For a moment he seems to have second thoughts about the harm he may bring to Gretchen, but Mephistopheles quickly keeps him from thinking about that.

The song Gretchen sings about the faithful lover is one of Goethe's most famous poems and was set to music by Romantic composers such as Franz Liszt and Hector Belioz. Another of Gretchen's songs, the spinning song from "Gretchen's Chamber," Part I, is equally famous and was set to music by Franz Schubert.

ON A WALK

Gretchen has been persuaded by her mother and the local priest to give the jewels to the Church, thus making Mephistopheles furious and giving Goethe a chance to make fun of the greed of the Church's servants. You discover that Faust's "second thoughts" in Gretchen's room were not very sincere. Gretchen's mother and the Church have given him a chance to abandon his evil plan. He decides to go ahead, however, and commands Mephistopheles not only to get another set of jewels, but also to reach Gretchen through her neighbor.

THE NEIGHBOR'S HOUSE

This is the first scene in which Faust does not appear. Mephistopheles shows what a good job he can do for his master, and the scene plays very well. It's funny, surprising, and full of comic devices. Mephistopheles invents a character for himself and carries it off so convincingly that he's afraid the widow Martha is falling for him. The scene also shows Gretchen beginning to give in to the Devil's seduction. With the help of Martha, she keeps the second casket of jewels concealed from her mother.

STREET

Look carefully at this little scene to understand Faust's development. At first, Faust makes moral objections to Mephistopheles' suggestion that he should pretend he was a witness to the death of Martha's husband, but then he has to admit he intends to deceive Gretchen. Faust tries to argue that his intense feelings are reason enough for pursuing Gretchen. In the end, however, he admits that the Devil is right.

GARDEN; GARDEN PAVILION

In these two scenes Gretchen reaches the peak of happiness. Faust declares his love for her as they are plucking the petals off a daisy, and she in turn declares her love for him in the little garden pavilion where he has pursued her. Faust has won her confidence by listening sympathetically to her life story. You now know more about Gretchen, especially about her relationship to her mother. This knowledge will explain Gretchen's later actions, which might otherwise seem inexcusable.

This scene is sometimes called the "quartet." As first Gretchen and Faust walk across the stage, then Martha and Mephistopheles, you see clearly the contrast between spiritualism and idealism (represented by Gretchen and Faust) and cynicism and materialism (represented by Martha and Mephistopheles).

FOREST AND CAVE

This scene is an interlude in the progress of the Gretchen drama. It is outside the realistic time frame that has been set up. The scene focuses on Faust's feelings—you might say it's a glimpse into his mind. In his first monologue, Faust had addressed the Earth Spirit, which rejected him. He now feels that the Spirit has blessed him with insight into himself and into living things. It seems as if the experience of love has reconciled Faust to the Earth Spirit, so that he feels in harmony with Nature.

Faust is beginning to hate Mephistopheles. He can't do without him, but he cannot stand his denial of strong emotions. Faust senses that his dependence on Mephistopheles will intensify as the Devil fulfills his desires and whets Faust's appetite for new experiences.

NOTE: You will have noticed that Faust's speech is in blank verse—that is five-stress lines that do not rhyme. It's the meter of Milton's *Paradise Lost* and of Shakespeare. Goethe deeply admired Shakespeare's works, which he read in English and in German translation. You will see the growing influence of Shakespeare as Part I comes to a close.

The rest of the scene illustrates what Faust is beginning to hate so much about Mephistopheles—the Devil's contempt for both Faust and Gretchen, his lack of respect for intense feelings, and his coarseness. Perhaps most irritating of all to Faust is that he has to admit Mephistopheles is right about his relationship to Gretchen. Gretchen must be a sacrifice to the powers of Hell, and this knowledge inevitably shatters Faust's mood of harmony with the Earth Spirit. As Mephistopheles speaks to Faust, he makes so many erotic references to Gretchen that Faust hurries away to find her.

GRETCHEN'S CHAMBER; MARTHA'S GARDEN

Remember that Faust and Gretchen have had no opportunity to consummate their love yet. In her sad song over the spinning wheel, Gretchen mourns for her lost peace of mind. Now that she is in love with Faust, her entire universe has been reduced to her relationship with him. Love brings joy only in the presence of the beloved. When he is not there, her heart aches.

Once you have seen the emotional states of both Faust and Gretchen, you see them together again in Martha's garden. The carefree young girl expressing her love has been replaced by a woman worrying over the spiritual health of her lover. Perhaps Gretchen is beginning to understand that Faust may not be trustworthy, since he does not accept the Christian faith. He answers her questions with a theological argument: God is indifferent about our belief in Him; it is enough that He gave us the capacity to relate emotionally to the world.

NOTE: Faust's reply to Gretchen goes beyond a speech appropriate to the character. It is an expression of Romantic theology. It does not matter whether we believe in God because God will perform His function in the universe without us and without the names we invent for Him. (Remember the Romantic preference for the idea and action behind the Word, not the Word itself.) Profound emotion sincerely felt represents an aspect of God. "Feeling is all," says Faust—or rather—Goethe.

Gretchen is consoled to some extent, though she now worries about Mephistopheles, whom she does not like. It was a common belief that the pure and innocent could sense the presence of the Devil, which Gretchen clearly does. She knows instinctively that Mephistopheles "cannot love a single soul." Faust, as you know from the previous scene, shares her feelings about Mephistopheles, yet he brushes her objections aside as prejudice.

It is a stroke of psychological genius to place the

consummation of Faust and Gretchen's love at a point where the relationship is troubled. Gretchen is insecure enough to agree to give her mother a sleeping potion. Despite what you have been told by Gretchen herself about her mother's harshness toward her, it is unlikely she would agree to risk her mother's life if she weren't desperately in love.

The final exchange between Faust and Mephistopheles shows the Devil mocking Gretchen's simple Christianity and looking forward to sharing Faust's sexual pleasure. He also anticipates trapping the souls of Faust and Gretchen and thereby winning his bet with God. His coarse and crude expression disgusts Faust, who is by now tormented with conflicting feelings.

AT THE WELL; BY THE CITY WALL

These two scenes confirm what you might have expected—Gretchen is pregnant by Faust. She faces the public shame that her companion at the well—Lieschen—describes with such relish for the girl they are gossiping about, and she seeks comfort for her anxiety and suffering from the Virgin Mary.

NIGHT

A cruel punishment is dealt Gretchen in this scene, where Faust and Gretchen's brother Valentine fight, and Valentine is killed. Not only does Gretchen lose a brother, but he dies cursing her.

Valentine's vehemence seems out of proportion until you remember from his first speech how much his own honor and reputation had been bound up with Gretchen's virtue. Valentine cares nothing at all for her feelings—a dying brother's curse is an unbearable burden—but only for the injury done to him: "When you renounced your honor first, Then was my heart most sorely pierced."

NOTE: Notice the song Mephistopheles sings as he and Faust approach Gretchen's house. It is a cruel song in which he mocks Gretchen. He sings that a girl shouldn't make love with a man unless she has a wedding ring from him.

What are your feelings toward Faust at this point? Do you find it difficult to see him as a victim of the Devil's magic? Remember that he has contributed to the deaths of Gretchen's mother and brother, and that in this scene he speaks of Gretchen with indifference, as if she were a prostitute.

CATHEDRAL

This is the last time you will see Gretchen as a sane girl. She is tormented by spirits—the voice of her own conscience—whose accusations are intensified by the Latin verses ["Day of Wrath"] sung by the choir during the Mass for her mother and brother. She is now totally ruined. Her mother has died as a result of the sleeping potion that Faust gave her; she is partly responsible for her brother's death; and she is pregnant by Faust, who has abandoned her.

NOTE: You'll have to make up your own mind about what caused Gretchen's ruin. It's too simple to say that it was caused by Mephistopheles' tricks. Although he brought Faust and Gretchen together and supplied the jewels and the sleeping potion, he did so on Faust's orders. Did Faust, then, cause Gretchen's misery? In one way he did, because he slept with her. But he could not have done so if she had remained as firm in her refusal as she was when she first met him. There are other, less direct causes: The doctrine of Romantic feeling so eloquently expressed by Faust apparently leads to disaster after the feelings are indulged. The society in which Gretchen lives is harsh and unforgiving, as the scene with Valentine illustrates so horribly. (In order to make a social criticism, Goethe probably based the Gretchen tragedy on the execution for infanticide of a girl in his native Frankfurt.)

WALPURGIS NIGHT

As Mephistopheles and Faust were skulking under Gretchen's window in Night, they were discussing their intention to attend the Witches' Sabbath, or Walpurgis Night. Walpurgis Night, April 30, celebrates May Day (May 1) and takes place in the Harz Mountains in central Germany. It is traditionally a night when witches gather on a high mountain for crude, sexually explicit celebrations.

Walpurgis Night represents Faust's deepest involvement with the Devil and his followers. In order to intensify your perception of Faust's degradation, Goethe has Walpurgis Night follow the scene where Gretchen, Faust's victim, faints in the Cathedral. Instead of showing you what Gretchen, in her madness, has suffered, he shows you how far Faust has fallen. The Walpurgis Night scene also gives you a sense of the unreality of the world Faust has entered through Mephistopheles' magic. Faust is not aware of Gretchen's pregnancy. Since she has killed the baby by the time he returns, he must have been gone about a year. The Walpurgis celebrations represent symbolically the way in which Faust passed his time during the year.

You should read the Walpurgis Night scene without worrying too much about the obscure references. Goethe put his enemies among the witches and made jokes about them that are difficult to understand now. The important thing to remember is that this is a Northern Witches' Sabbath, in contrast to the Classical Walpurgis Night in Part II. Goethe is fascinated by the contrast between the gloomy Romantic North, represented by Germany and the sunny Classical South, represented by Greece.

Mephistopheles and Faust journey to the mountain, led by an erratic Will-o'-the-Wisp, while overhead the witches fly in on the storm winds. They make such noisy confusion when they land and greet each other that Mephistopheles pulls Faust aside. He thinks it odd they should isolate themselves from what they came to see, but Mephistopheles offers him a tour of the groups assembled round their different fires.

They visit a group of old men bemoaning modern times (these may have been modeled on Goethe's colleagues in the government of Weimar). Then they dance with witches to the accompaniment of lewd jokes.

Suddenly, the fun goes sour for Faust. First, he finds himself disgusted with his dancing partner, a pretty young witch, because a mouse jumps out of her mouth as they dance together. Then, he sees an apparition that reminds him of Gretchen. He cannot take his eyes from her, gazing with horror at a thin red line across her throat. You can imagine Mephistopheles realizing that he must do something quickly or Faust will turn and run away. He grabs Faust and pulls him along to see a play that is just about to be performed.

WALPURGIS NIGHT'S DREAM

The play with which Mephistopheles distracts Faust serves as an interlude and has no real connection with the rest of the play. There is no plot and nothing happens. The scene is called "The Golden Wedding of Oberon and Titania" and refers directly to Shakespeare's *A Midsummer Night's Dream*. The four-line poems are recited by mythological characters and various other strange figures and most make fun of Goethe's contemporaries. This interlude serves as a transition between the frenzied Walpurgis Night celebration and the scene that will follow.

DREARY DAY

This is the only scene in *Faust* written in prose rather than verse. Why does Goethe's style change here? Some readers believe Goethe switched to prose to highlight Faust's return to the real world from the fanciful world of Walpurgis Night.

Faust is filled with anger and guilt. He learns that Gretchen is in prison and he accuses Mephistopheles of deliberately distracting him while

Gretchen suffered. He asks Mephistopheles to help
him free her, but the Devil refuses. After Faust
finishes shouting at him, Mephistopheles accuses
Faust of lacking the courage to accept the consequences of his actions. "Which one of us is most
responsible for Gretchen's ruin?" he asks. Mephistopheles becomes unaccountably less powerful
than Faust thought he was. "Do I have all the power
on earth and in heaven?" He can't release Gretchen
from prison, and he can't protect Faust from the
police, who are looking for him after Valentine's
murder. All he can do is trick the jailer so that
Faust can seize the prison keys and take Gretchen
away.

NIGHT; DUNGEON

Faust and Mephistopheles ride magic horses to
the dungeon where Gretchen lies imprisoned. On
the way, they pass the stone where she will be
beheaded (Faust had seen a red line round her
neck at the Walpurgis Night dance), and where
the witches are already gathering like vultures.

The dungeon scene is heart-rending. As Faust
approaches Gretchen's cell, he hears her singing
an insane song much like the one Ophelia sings in
Shakespeare's *Hamlet* (Act IV, scene v). She mistakes Faust for her executioner, and as she begs
him to save her, Faust realizes she is mad. Faust
is wracked with guilt, and as he calls her name,
she recognizes him.

Faust begs her to leave with him, but she refuses. In her confused state she rambles wildly about
her baby's drowning and her mother's death, and
about the details of the places where all the mem-

bers of her ruined family are to be buried. She knows she doesn't want to escape punishment for her sins and believes only death will bring her peace of mind. Faust almost picks her up to carry her away but her refusal to flee deters him. As day breaks, the bells begin to peal for her execution, but she thinks they are wedding bells.

This scene, which concludes Part I of *Faust*, ends in frenzied action. Mephistopheles tries to hurry Faust away, because the magic horses will disappear with daylight and they must be on their way. He pulls Faust away as Gretchen throws herself down in a final prayer. Mephistopheles coldly says she is condemned, but he is contradicted by a heavenly voice that announces, "Redeemed!" They leave as Gretchen calls Faust's name with her dying breath.

NOTE: Some readers believe that when Mephistopheles calls "Hither! To me!" he is dragging Faust away to Hell. Such an ending would be appropriate if Part I concluded the play. Certainly it creates a dramatic contrast between the heavenly voice redeeming Gretchen and the devilish one summoning Faust. You should take these last few lines into account when you argue for or against the unity of *Faust*.

This is not the last you will see of Gretchen. She appears at the end of the whole drama when she pleads for Faust's soul.

Faust has made a dismal failure of his first experiments with supernatural power. He has caused destruction and suffering to a whole family through the indulgence of his own feelings, aided by Mephistopheles' power. Yet perhaps he suffers more than all his victims, because he is left with the burden of guilt. Think back to the "Prologue in Heaven." The Lord said that man must always err while he strives. Faust has tried to satisfy his desires and has caused misery and destruction. But the Lord also had confidence that man understands the right way, no matter how dark his urges. Faust must now reconcile himself to the painful knowledge of "the appointed course."

PART II

In Part II of *Faust* the theme of striving also is important. You'll remember that at the end of Part I Faust was still not happy; he continues to need to satisfy his craving for worldly accomplishments and experiences. He will find that no experience or accomplishment will bring him lasting peace, but it is of utmost importance that he continue to strive, and that he believe there is something larger than himself.

Faust continues to have new experiences and adventures in Part II. His pact with Mephistopheles is still in effect and will be until Faust's death. A difference between the two parts is that in Part I, Goethe bombards you with intense physical experience, while Part II is calmer as it explores your Classical heritage. For that reason, Part II is more representative of mankind's (particularly Western man's) striving for fulfillment than of an individual's striving.

In Part II, Goethe creates a world of magic, filled

with symbolism. At times it will not seem to make sense. But don't worry, time and space are meaningless in this part of *Faust*. The important thing for you to keep in mind is Faust's striving, his grasping for understanding.

ACT I

CHARMING LANDSCAPE

The first scene acts as a bridge between Part I and Part II of *Faust*. Faust, perhaps shortly after the emotional scene in Gretchen's prison cell, is at the point of nervous collapse. As he tosses and turns in a bed of flowers, kind spirits sing him to sleep. The spirits are led by Ariel, the air sprite of Shakespeare's *The Tempest*. Ariel sings about forgetfulness and healing, and suggests that when Faust wakes he will feel refreshed.

NOTE: Because *Faust* is about the striving of Western man, and because Goethe praises artistic and intellectual attainments, you shouldn't be surprised that he modeled much of the poetry in this scene after the works of two other great writers, Dante and Shakespeare. Ariel's song is similar to Ariel's lines in Shakespeare's *The Tempest*. Ariel is the voice of the air who is released into nature in Shakespeare's play. In *Faust*, Ariel speaks as the healing voice of nature.

The meter of Faust's monologue is that used by Dante in the *Divine Comedy*. In the *Divine Comedy*, Dante travels from Hell to Heaven in search of understanding about God and salvation. The me-

ter Dante used was called terza rima (third rhyme)
and rhymed *aba, bcb, cdc,* and so on.

The final stanza of the poem is an elaborate hymn
to human life. Faust stands with the sun behind
him—knowledge too powerful for man—watching
a waterfall, which represents the rush of life. The
water breaks into innumerable streams, just like
the actions of men. But the downward force sends
up a spray, "a soaring lacework," whose droplets
make a rainbow. "This mirrors all aspiring human
action," says Faust. The shining prisms flung upward represent art, music, philosophy—the best
of human attainments. This is Faust's consolation.
No matter how terrible man's mistakes may be, he
is capable of the finest achievements.

IMPERIAL RESIDENCE

Remember that in the second Study scene of
Part I, Mephistopheles promised Faust that they
would peruse first the small world and then the
great. In this scene, you see the great world of the
Emperor's court. Most of the Faust legends include
a visit to the Emperor's court, where Faust as-
tounds the Emperor with magic tricks. But this one
is different. The Emperor is no single monarch but
a representative of monarchy in general. You will
notice that no one in this scene has a name, except
Mephistopheles. The people are all types—the
Chancellor (a high official, such as a secretary to a
king), the Treasurer, and so on. The problems they
complain of are universal. As Mephistopheles takes
his place beside the Emperor, the crowd mutters

its comments. Watch for these barely audible remarks throughout this scene and the next. They frequently express the commonsense view of what is going on.

The Emperor doesn't seem very interested in affairs of state. He wants to get on with a planned Carnival celebration (see the next scene), but his court officers paint a picture of a kingdom in ruin—lawless, in debt, its citizens demoralized.

NOTE: Goethe himself was a minister of state for the Duchy of Weimar and was familiar with court life and the administration of a country. He bases his generalizations about sound administration on his own experience, as you will also see when Mephistopheles brings paper money—and inflation—to the Emperor's court.

The Emperor's shallowness is shown by his turning to Mephistopheles, now dressed as the Court Fool, for his opinion. Mephistopheles answers with blatant flattery, which the crowd immediately recognizes. He promises the court vast stores of money to solve the realm's problems. The court officials, however, are not all as foolish as the Emperor. The Chancellor senses that he is in the presence of an evil power. Notice in his speech the number of references to the Devil: "Mind is Satan"; "The black magician!"; and, finally, "The wizard and the fool live hide in hide." But he is brushed aside and never speaks again during the scene. Foolish trust in trickery entrances the court as Mephistopheles manipulates an Astrologer to

promise hoards of gold and then describes how
much gold there is to be dug out of the ground.
    The Emperor is impatient to get the gold, but
Mephistopheles apparently needs time. He uses
the Astrologer as a mouthpiece to insist on the
normal course of events, especially the Carnival.
As the Emperor and his court take their places for
the Carnival, Mephistopheles contemptuously
scorns "This foolish lot."

SPACIOUS HALL

    This scene introduces Faust to the Emperor's
Court, and the Carnival (which you learn later was
directed by Faust) is a convenient opportunity for
Faust and Mephistopheles to dazzle the court with
magic. The entertainment is in the form of a masque,
a court spectacle in which music and dancing accompany a pageant of symbolic characters. The
Carnival, modeled on Roman carnivals that the
Emperor (and Goethe) had seen, celebrates Mardi
Gras, the Tuesday before the first day of Lent (Ash
Wednesday).
    The masque portion of the entertainment pro-
ceeds much as planned by the Herald, who acts
as the master of ceremonies and controls it from
the side of the stage. Mephistopheles and Faust
then give it a sinister turn, playing on the crowd's
fascination with gold and magic power. At the cul-
mination of the action, the entire stage bursts into
flames, which can be quenched only by water
magically produced—like the flames themselves—
by Faust.

Lines 5065–5455
The first part of the masque follows the Italian pat-
tern pretty closely, with flowers, flower girls, gar-

deners, woodcutters, and other rustic figures. The mood becomes comic as stock characters from Italian comedy enter, wearing baggy pants and traditional makeup. There is a general drinking chorus, which leads into a procession of poets. At this point the masque becomes explicitly Classical. The Herald introduces, in turn, the three Graces, the three Fates, and the three Furies, who describe their respective functions. The climax of the masque comes with the entrance of Victory on the elephant.

Lines 5456–5986
With the entry of Mephistopheles, dressed as two vulgar characters from Greek literature, the Herald loses his grip on the pageant. When he strikes Mephistopheles with his stick, the Devil becomes first an egg, then a snake, and then a bat, alarming the spectators, who scatter in fear.

The Herald is reduced to asking for help in order to explain the chariot which now appears. It is driven by a boy who represents poetry, and carries Faust, disguised as Plutus, the god of wealth. Mephistopheles now personifies Greed, one of the seven deadly sins in medieval Christian belief.

The boy charioteer's tricks with jewelry and flames, and Mephistopheles' disguise, indicate the theme—greed for gold. Faust, as Plutus, shows great chests of gold to the crowd, who try to rush for them. They are beaten back, however, by flames from the Herald's mace (a club; sometimes a symbol of authority), magically produced by Faust.

Mephistopheles transforms the gold into a giant male sexual symbol. The Emperor and his lords enter, dressed as the Greek god Pan (who ruled over nature) and his followers, bringing with them the expectation of unrestrained indulgence in sensual pleasure and the threat of uncontrolled violence.

Finally, everything goes up in flames as the Emperor's beard catches fire. You can imagine the Herald standing to one side, describing the horror of the scene as the entire hall lights up. Faust magically douses the flames with water, bringing calm to a terrible scene.

NOTE: Does the light-hearted Carnival depict the tone of the Emperor's court? Does the masque represent the self-indulgence of the court? The Emperor, responsible for an entire kingdom, seems only to be interested in entertainment. Is Goethe suggesting that this is true of all Emperors? What is the significance of the references to Greek mythology? Is it to differentiate the Romantic [Germanic] world, in which the mood is serious, and the more light-hearted Classical [Italian] world? The fact that the boy charioteer (who represents poetry) accompanies Plutus (the god of wealth) may suggest that poetry adds spiritual meaning to the comforts of material wealth. Faust's and Mephistopheles' use of gold and fire, important to the survival of any society, might suggest that if these elements are not handled properly, they can destroy the society that needs them.

PLEASANCE

Because of their brilliant success with the Carnival Masque, Faust and Mephistopheles are in great favor at court. The Emperor even orders Faust to secure all future entertainments. Mephistopheles and Faust further prove their usefulness when the court officials rush in, declaring that all the problems of the kingdom have been solved by the introduction of paper money. Even the skeptical Chancellor seems convinced as he reads a proclamation that the paper currency represents gold waiting to be mined.

Mephistopheles sounds like a huckster peddling a new gadget as he describes the convenience of paper money. Faust is more serious, pointing out that because the paper money is based on gold, it is secure. The light-minded Emperor believes them both and rewards them with the "inner soil" of his realm, the ground beneath the surface where the gold is supposedly hidden. He gives paper money to all his courtiers, who promptly exit to spend it on their own concerns.

NOTE: Goethe's original audience would have been more interested in the problems caused by paper money than you might be. Paper money had been introduced in France in the eighteenth century, and Louis XV's use of it (and the subsequent inflation it caused) helped create the financial crisis that contributed to the French Revolution. The French Revolutionary government had also used paper money, which became practically worthless in just a few years. Because this entire episode with the Emperor is a satire, do you think Goethe might be poking fun at those who thought that the introduction of paper money would solve all their problems? Could Goethe be pointing out the greed of the Emperor, his officials, and his subjects? Don't forget that all of the circumstances surrounding the issuance of paper money at the Emperor's court are magical and therefore fraudulent. It is Mephistopheles who devised the plan and the Emperor's signature had been obtained the night before at the Carnival, where he had been unaware of what he was signing.

DARK GALLERY

Faust is beginning to find the Emperor's constant demands for amusement trying. Now he must produce Helen of Troy and her lover, Paris, who stole her from her Greek husband, King Menelaus of Sparta, and thus provoked the Trojan War.

Mephistopheles can't help Faust much. Notice that when Faust faces a crisis, Mephistopheles backs off. In Part I, his magic could not save Gretchen, and now he contends, "I have no commerce with that pagan clutter"—an excuse that depends on Mephistopheles' origins in Christianity. The only way Mephistopheles can show Faust is through an encounter with mythic figures called the Mothers. Faust must descend into the underworld, where the Mothers live, with a magic key in his hand. He will see a tripod (three-legged stool) in the middle of the Mothers; he must touch the key to the tripod and bring it back. The key will then have the power to summon mythological characters.

NOTE: This adventure will differ from Faust's previous ones. The influence of the Devil is less evident as Faust moves from the world of flesh and blood to that of spirits. Mephistopheles tells him that he must reach into emptiness and limitless space to find what he's looking for. Some readers think this scene illustrates the limits and superficiality of Christianity. Do you think Goethe is arguing that Christianity has no power over the basic elements of life?

The Mothers seem to be Goethe's own invention. He suggested in a letter that they might be based on a cult of mother goddesses found in Chapter 20, "The Life of Marcellus," of Plutarch's *Lives*. Some readers think Goethe might be punning on the similarity in sound between the German words for mother ("Mutter") and myth ("Mythe"). No matter where Goethe got the idea for the Mothers, they seem to represent something primeval, the source of all life.

BRIGHTLY LIT BALLROOMS

In this light and cheerful scene, Mephistopheles stalls while Faust goes down to the Mothers. Mephistopheles is helped by the court ladies, who want his magic powers to help them cure freckles and a lame foot, as well as to recover a straying lover. Mephistopheles is losing his usual confidence. He prays to the Mothers to let Faust go and then looks fearfully into the Hall of Chivalry, where the Emperor and his court are assembling. The hall is dark and mysterious enough to frighten even Mephistopheles with spirits that "find their way all by themselves."

HALL OF CHIVALRY

Chivalry refers to the medieval code of knightly conduct, which includes courage, loyalty, courtesy, fairness, respect for women, and protection of the poor.

This is one of the most theatrical scenes in *Faust*. Imagine the stage in two parts: an inner stage on which Faust, who has just returned from the Mothers, presents Paris and Helen; and an outer one, where the Emperor and his court are arranged on each side, watching the action and at the same time addressing their remarks to each other and to the audience. The fun in this scene comes from the chatter of the court ladies and gentlemen as they criticize the apparitions of Paris and Helen, treating them as if they were real people, almost their colleagues at court. Contrast this chatter with the deep reverence of Faust, who is stirred to his soul by Helen's beauty. The action cuts from one to the other as the tension mounts.

When Helen emerges, Mephistopheles shows his coarseness in his comment: "She's pretty, yes, but not my cup of tea." Nevertheless, Faust is overwhelmed.

NOTE: From its beginning, the Faust story included the raising of Helen from the underworld. It is regarded as the ultimate magic trick. Marlowe's *Doctor Faustus* contains a famous line spoken by Faust as he first sees Helen: "Is this the face that launched a thousand ships?" This is, of course, a reference to Helen's central role as the cause of the Trojan War, according to the ancient Greek epic *The Iliad* by Homer.

The magical appearance of Helen is especially important in understanding Faust's quest. She represents the essence of female beauty, eternal and always guarding its ultimate mystery. She is also a Classical heroine, who brings with her the authority of great poetry from the age of Homer. But this Helen is a "shade," a reflection of real beauty. Faust wants to acquire the real Helen, not the apparition in this scene. His pursuit of Helen symbolizes Faust's desire to unite in himself the Classical and the Romantic spirits.

Look carefully at the terms by which Faust worships Helen, so that you can understand the difference in his attitude toward Gretchen in Part I and Helen in Part II. He sees Helen as the ideal of beauty that he could only imagine "deep within my breast." He felt mostly lust for Gretchen and he had treated her indifferently. Seeing Helen marks a watershed in his life. From here on, he will take on a "new priesthood," worshipping Helen and undertaking a "dread quest" in search of her. In pursuing Helen and vowing to devote the energies of sexual passion to her, Faust is trying to unite the ideal, or Classical (symbolized by Helen), and the real, or Romantic (symbolized by passion). You will see that ultimately he fails. Excess emotion brings ruin and grief.

As the apparition of Helen approaches the sleeping Paris, you follow the action through the comments of the watching courtiers. But Faust has become obsessed. He tries to rescue Helen as Paris sweeps her up in his arms, flourishes his magic key at the apparition, and invokes the Mothers to

help him gain what he cannot live without. The
crowd of courtiers rise from their seats terrified as
a loud explosion ends the show. Faust loses con-
sciousness and is carried off by Mephistopheles.

ACT II

Goethe has to bring Faust and Helen together.
Faust is still far from his goals, but he will have to
find new ways of reaching them. In his search for
the reality that the shade of Helen represents, Faust
must go to the world of Persephone, the queen of
the underworld. As you already know, Mephistopheles can't lead Faust into the world of the
spirits of Classical antiquity, so Homunculus ("little man"), a spirit in a glass bottle, will be his guide.
Mephistopheles, Faust, and Homunculus will,
through participation in a Classical Walpurgis Night,
enter into the Classical world. Homunculus finds
bodily life by jumping into the ocean, Mephistopheles finds a new disguise, and Faust finds a spirit
that will lead him to the underworld. The first two
scenes of Act II serve as a transition from the Emperor's court to the Classical Walpurgis Night.

NARROW, HIGH-VAULTED
GOTHIC CHAMBER

Mephistopheles has taken Faust, unconscious,
back to his original study and the Romantic Gothic
gloom. It all remains exactly the same as it was
four years earlier—four years, because the student
who asked Mephistopheles' advice then is now a
graduate. You will realize the point of returning to
the study when you notice the contrast between

the dull, unchanged life there and the profound changes that experience has brought to Faust himself.

Goethe's sense of fun is never far away. As Mephistopheles shakes out Faust's fur gown, a cloud of insects rises from it. They burst into song, calling Mephistopheles their father!

Mephistopheles wants someone to recognize that he is "the Dean," in his moth-eaten fur robe. So he pulls the bell, which literally threatens to shake the whole place apart and symbolically signals a new era in Faust's old study.

The first visitor is a replacement for Wagner, who has now become a doctor. The famulus (student) stresses that everything has been preserved as Faust had left it, thus preparing you for the entrance of the Baccalaureus. Impressed with his own accomplishments, the formerly timid student now scorns the "pickled wisdom" of his teachers and calls himself "a different specimen."

He attacks Mephistopheles—whom he thinks is the professor because he is wearing the moth-eaten old gown—until Mephistopheles edges away from him. You'll probably be surprised to hear the Baccalaureus say: "One who is thirty years or older/ Already is as good as dead." Mephistopheles mutters in reply that one has to be old (experienced) to understand the Devil.

LABORATORY

The bell that shook the building signals success for Dr. Wagner in his labortory. He has been trying to produce human life in a test tube, but as you

might expect from his plodding character in
Part I, Wagner lacks creative genius.

Mephistopheles' appearance provides the creative spark Wagner needs. As he arrives, a tiny human figure takes shape in the test tube, and the
Homunculus speaks to Wagner, his "father," and
to Mephistopheles, his "cousin."

NOTE: Homunculus, which means "little man,"
owes part of his origin to Goethe's interest in alchemy and early science, which was just as concerned with the creation of life as with the chang-
ing of lead into gold. He represents pure spirit or
mind without shape or form, and this makes him
independent of Mephistopheles. This pure spirit,
who leads Faust into the Classical world, seeks to
become material, to be alive within the world of
nature. Do you find his search comparable to that
of Faust? Some readers suggest that Homunculus
represents intellect, others the vital life-spirit in man.
Whatever he represents, like Faust he is driven by
an intense desire to find the secrets of the universe.

Homunculus eavesdrops on Faust's dream of
Leda and the Swan and suggests taking him to
Classical Walpurgis Night. Classical Walpurgis
Night, he says, is joyous and reflects southern Europe (remember that Goethe had recently returned
from a trip to Italy), whereas the Germanic (Romantic) Walpurgis Night is indicative of the gloomy
north. Mephistopheles has never heard of such an
event and is not certain he wants to attend, but
when Homunculus describes some of the erotic

pleasures he will experience, the Devil decides to
go. Mephistopheles lifts Faust and follows Homunculus.

In Greek myth, Helen—whose abduction by Paris
caused the Trojan War—was the daughter of Leda
and Zeus, the supreme god of the Greeks. Zeus
made Leda pregnant when he took the form of a
swan. Thus, Helen had more than earthly beauty
because her father was a god.

CLASSICAL WALPURGIS NIGHT

You are now facing about 1480 lines of poetry
containing many names that you may not have
heard before. Don't be put off by all the classical
allusions. Even readers with a wide knowledge of
Greek literature will find many of Goethe's mythological figures obscure, because he alludes to research and theories about early Greek religion that
were current in the late eighteenth century and
have been disproved since.

As a guide, remember that Mephistopheles,
Faust, and Homunculus are all seeking something
in these scenes, and you follow each of them in
turn. Faust is seeking Helen, so you can monitor
the thread of his search. Mephistopheles is looking
for a figure—the more horrible the better—whose
shape he can borrow for a disguise. Homunculus
is trying to become a person; his search ends in
the spectacular climax to the Classical Walpurgis
Night, which becomes a great song of praise to the
sea as the origin of life.

THE PHARSALIAN FIELDS

As you read this scene, compare it with the similar one introducing the Walpurgis Night in Part I. In the Classical Walpurgis Night, Erichtho, an ugly enchantress, describes the scene and explains why the celebration begins on the field of Pharsalus, in Thessaly, where Caesar defeated Pompey in 48 B.C., thus paving the way for the creation of the Roman Empire. Here, where the ancient world yielded to the modern one, the mythological creatures gather annually to remember their former glory. Here, too, and on this night, Faust will find a way into that earlier world.

Watch for the parallels between the two Walpurgis Nights. Each needs a light to guide visitors. In Germany, however, the light is an erratic Will-o'-the-Wisp, and here the light, from Homunculus' test tube, is so bright that Erichtho thinks it is a meteor. In the first Walpurgis Night, Mephistopheles conducts Faust around the fires, but here he suggests that "each should range the fires alone" and then meet again when Homunculus flashes his light.

Mephistopheles sets Faust on his feet, and Faust immediately asks where Helen is. He is renewed, refreshed by standing on Greek soil and breathing the air that "spoke her native tongue."

ON THE UPPER PENEIOS

This is a humorous scene, in which Mephistopheles exchanges riddles with sphinxes and teases the griffins. His approach to the mythological creatures is quite different from that of Faust, who acts

like a visitor to a museum, connecting the exhibits
to his reading.

When Faust asks the sphinxes about Helen, they
tell him that, historically, she is more recent than
they are, so they don't know anything about her.
They refer him to Chiron the Centaur, who, half-
man and half-horse, will be found prancing around
at the Walpurgis Night. He can tell Faust about
Helen, because he tutored her half-brothers.

ON THE LOWER PENEIOS

In this scene, Faust succeeds in his search for a
way down to Helen in the underworld. As the
scene begins, Faust is listening to the noises of the
water lapping on the banks of the river Peneios.
He then looks across the river and sees the same
scene he dreamed of while lying unconscious in
his old study. The maidens are bathing with Leda
when Zeus approaches in the form of a swan. The
other swans distract the maidens' attention while
Zeus makes love to Leda.

Chiron appears and invites Faust to ride on his
back. As conceived by Goethe, Chiron is a level-
headed fellow, an old schoolmaster who knows
what to expect and how to judge character. He
remembers with special pleasure how young Helen
thanked him for saving her life: "So charming—
young, an old man's joy—was she!" He thinks Faust
is a little carried away with passion, so he offers
to introduce him to Manto, a sorceress with magic
healing powers.

When they arrive at her temple, Chiron and
Manto exchange affectionate greetings, as they do
each year (remember, this is a reunion of old gods

and demigods). After committing Faust to Manto's care, Chiron is off again. Manto understands at once what Faust needs. She leads him to the entrance of the underworld and pushes him through, as she did with Orpheus when he was seeking Eurydice.

While the rest of the Walpurgis Night continues above ground, Faust is in the underworld releasing Helen fromPersephone's reign. You won't find this out until Act III, but you should be aware of the simultaneous action because it helps you to understand what happens to Homunculus.

ON THE UPPER PENEIOS, AS BEFORE

Meanwhile, on the Upper Peneios River, an earthquake, Seismos, is giving birth to a mountain, in a comic scene that is intended to lighten the atmosphere after the intensity of Faust's passion.

Mephistopheles is stumbling around trying to return to the sphinxes when he comes upon Homunculus, "Sparkleface." Homunculus is desperately trying to find help in "becoming": "I cannot wait to smash my glass and flare." He is following Thales and Anaxagoras—two important Greek philosophers of the sixth and fifth centuries B.C.—whom he thinks will be able to advise him, although Mephistopheles tells him to trust his own efforts instead.

Still grumbling about the inferiority of these mountains to his German ones, Mephistopheles stumbles onto the cave of the Graeae, whom he calls the Phorcyads (three daughters of Phorcys, an old sea god, and Ceto; in Greek, *graeae* means "old women," or, as in this instance, "old hags").

They are the most horrifying witches of all, living in complete darkness and passing among them a single eye and a single tooth. Mephistopheles' humor never deserts him. Calling himself a "far relation" of the Phorcyads, he asks permission to approach as he falls "silent now in ecstasy" and continues to flatter them in the most disgusting terms. Mephistopheles seems to find satisfaction only with the ugly spirits.

It is no wonder that they agree to let him assume their shape and even show him how to twist his face to look like them: "Just close one eye, 'twill do it even so." Apparently, he has lent them one of his eyes and a tooth in exchange, for they are left chuckling with witchlike glee over their extra organs.

ROCKY INLETS
OF THE AEGEAN SEA

This scene belongs to Homunculus. Thales guides Homunculus to Nereus (son of Pontus, the deep sea, and Mother Earth), calling him a "cantankerous old vinegar-crock." Like Chiron, Nereus is given a recognizable character by Goethe. He complains at length that no one takes his advice, which could have saved the world several disasters, including the Trojan War.

From the cliffs, the Sirens see that the sea nymphs are bringing the ancient Cabiri, whose number seems a bit uncertain. Homunculus doesn't think much of the Cabiri, but Thales remarks that anything ancient is highly prized. Proteus thinks he'll play games with them and changes his shape several times, until he sees Homunculus. Proteus doesn't hesitate to urge Homunculus to begin his life in the sea.

From the cliffs, Nereus and Thales watch the procession on the waves below. Nereus' daughters, the Dorids, float by with their sailor lovers, and then Galatea, a goddess of beauty, appears. You will marvel at the beauty of this scene. Nereus greets his daughter just this once each year. It is one of those moments of intense life for which Faust yearns, a moment worth all the others: "Yet a single loving gaze/All the empty year outweighs." The procession goes far out to sea, as Nereus and Thales struggle to catch a glimpse of "Galatea's throne . . . shell-bedecked." Homunculus greets the "lovely damp," and then, as Thales reports the action to Nereus, Homunculus crashes his test tube at Galatea's feet. Blinding light fills the whole scene as fire, earth, air, and water mingle in the unity of creation.

Magnificent though it is, Homunculus' end leaves a pang of loss. But he is no longer necessary, for at this moment Faust has released Helen from the underworld. The celebration by the Aegean Sea marks the beginning of life for Helen, born again through Faust's love.

ACT III

To help understand Act III, you should review the Walpurgis Night in Part I. It is followed immediately by the Walpurgis Night's Dream, a satyr play. You will see the parallel with the Classical Walpurgis Night, which is followed by this act, written in the form of a Greek tragedy. A satyr play, ribald and coarse, suited the Walpurgis Night's activities. A Greek tragedy is poetic and sublime, a fitting sequel to the Classical Walpurgis Night.

You get a bonus from Act III, known as the Helen Act, because you'll learn about the form of Greek tragedy as you read it. The first part is an exact imitation of a play by the Greek dramatist Euripides, even to the meter of the verse.

Greek tragedy does not set out to be realistic. It has formal rules: there should be no more than three actors in a scene (usually only two); most of the action should take place off stage, reported in long formal speeches, with many references to mythological figures; and there should be a chorus. The chorus is both involved in the action and a commentator on it. The members of the chorus are often citizens or servants, people whose lives will be affected by what happens to the kings, queens, and heroes who are the leading figures in the tragedy.

BEFORE THE PALACE OF MENELAUS AT SPARTA

Lines 8488–8696
You find Helen before the doors of her own palace in Sparta. The Trojan War is over after ten years of fighting, and Helen has been brought back by her husband, Menelaus, king of Sparta. There is no sign that Helen knows she has just been released from the underworld by Faust. The action has shifted back to the times of ancient Greece.

Helen goes into Menelaus' palace, "long missed and longed-for much," while the Chorus praises the gods for Helen's return to Sparta. But Helen rushes back onto the stage, horrified at what she

has found. Crouched beside the fireplace is Phorcyas, who, you will remember, is Mephistopheles
in disguise. Read Helen's speech aloud to experience the horror of Phorcyas, who has only one eye
and one tooth and is "Of stature gaunt, and hol-
low, bloody-blear of eye."

Lines 8697–8881

You can imagine the dramatic shock of seeing
the dreadful figure of Phorcyas/Mephistopheles,
wrapped in gray rags, with a hideous face shrouded
by a hood. The Chorus is deeply shaken and iden-
tifies the monster, correctly, as one of "Phorcys'
daughters," which provokes a furious retort from
Phorcyas.

   You should remember that Phorcyas is a woman,
while Mephistopheles is a man—or at least has
male form. Just to remind you whom we're talking
about, the pronoun "he" will be used for Phorcyas.

   Helen defends the Chorus with dignity, but
Phorcyas turns his fury on her, telling her that, if
she's mistress of the palace, she should do her job
and keep her serving women in order. The quarrel
develops into a slanging match, which takes the
form of stichomythia, a component of Greek tragedy in which the combatants take one line each.
The tension increases with each line until Helen
intervenes, distraught.

   The noise and the furious feelings have diso-
riented Helen. Now, for the first time, she has some
hint that she may have been in the underworld.
She turns to Phorcyas, sensing that the monster
has the authority of a mythical creature that moves
between the human and the mythical spheres.

Phorcyas and Helen begin a dialogue, two lines each, which recounts Helen's past history.

NOTE: You may be a bit confused by all the events that seem to have happened to one woman. Helen was the most beautiful woman in the world, so it was natural to associate her with every hero from Theseus to Achilles. One story regarding Helen and the Greek hero of the Trojan War, Achilles, said that after death, Helen and Achilles met on the island of Leuce, in the Black Sea, and there produced a son, Euphorion. Myths about Helen are basically folk tales, as are most of the Greek legends. They arise in different places and tend to be associated with a famous name. You can see myth-making in action in your own social group, school, or college. An outstanding person is frequently discussed and stories are told about him or her. Before long, it becomes impossible to separate the truth from what is commonly said about the person.

The discussion of her past has made Helen even more unsure of her own reality. She faints, unable to face the dizzying sense that she has become a myth to herself.

Lines 8882–9126
The Chorus tends Helen, reproaching Phorcyas for the unintended effect of digging up the past. There is worse news to come about the future. Helen has been puzzled about the lack of a sacrificial animal for the ceremony she has been told to prepare.

Now Phorcyas tells her that she, Helen, is to be killed for the sacrifice. As the Chorus and Helen stand transfixed with horror, Phorcyas summons his nasty little dwarves, who prepare the sacrifice, making the details even more vivid.

All this is Phorcyas/Mephistopheles' way of presenting Faust as Helen's rescuer. In his next speeches, he spans a thousand years of time to bring together Homeric Helen and the Crusaders, who built castles in Greece on their way to the Holy Land.

Helen has only to command, says Mephistopheles, and she will be safe in one of the castles. But she cannot believe that Menelaus will harm her. Phorcyas not only tells him more tales of horror but also arranges for a trumpet to sound, convincing Helen and the Chorus that Menelaus is coming. There is a dramatic pause. Everything on stage is silent and still. Then, Helen decides. Although she senses that Phorcyas is "a froward demon" and that everything may not be pleasant in the future, she will go to the castle.

INNER COURTYARD OF A CASTLE

Lines 9127–9356
As they enter the castle, their spirits rise. The mist clears, and Phorcyas has gone. They enjoy their welcome, as servants prepare a throne and canopy for Helen. When Faust appears—for the first time in this act—he is dressed as a knight at court, with a long cloak covering ceremonial armor.

NOTE: Anachronism, the placing of historical events in the wrong time period, is usually considered a fault. But the mixing of historical periods is one of the glories of *Faust*. Here you have a legendary figure from Homeric Greece meeting a Renaissance scholar in a medieval castle with knights in armor! Such a mingling of times, places, and people can happen only in the imagination. A new entity is created. This scene also provides a transition from the world of antiquity to the world of Faust.

Observe how cleverly Goethe sets up the first encounter between Helen and Faust. Faust drags before her a watchman, Lynceus (the lynx-eyed pilot of the ship *Argos* in Greek mythology), who was supposed to warn Faust of Helen's approach so that he could greet her properly. Helen asks Lynceus to speak in his own defense, and he replies with a medieval ballad of love, a lyrical poem to Helen's beauty, which blinded him so that he forgot his duty.

Of course, Helen forgives Lynceus. Faust then expresses his own devotion to her: "What choice have I but to consign myself,/And all I owned in fancy, unto thee?" Lynceus' song accompanies the presentation of all the jewels he accumulated during the battles the Crusaders fought, but Faust will not allow him to leave them at Helen's feet. Instead, Lynceus must adorn the interior of the castle so that it shines in "supreme lucence" (light). Lynceus' final speech sums up the reaction of all men to Helen's beauty—the sun is wan and cold in comparison with it.

NOTE: Some readers argue that Faust, in this scene, represents the northern (barbarian) conqueror who destroyed Greek civilization. Others argue that he symbolizes the northern peoples who absorbed Classical culture during the Renaissance. What do you think?

Lines 9357–9573
In this scene, Helen and Faust are symbolically united. You could say that it is one of the high points, perhaps the highest point, of the drama. It's a scene of joy and laughter. It begins with Helen asking Faust about rhyme. He teaches her how to do it, and, of course, they make love to each other as they rhyme. This symbolizes the union of the Classical style, which did not have rhyme, and the Romantic style, which used rhyme in the simple poems imitated from folk poetry. Notice how calm and relaxed this scene is. Faust is no longer on a frantic quest. His striving is now directed toward more down-to-earth goals.

Lines 9574–9678
While they are secluded, protected by Phorcyas, Faust and Helen produce a child, Euphorion. The birth and development of this fairy child are described by Phorcyas, who tells a story of his apparent disappearance and then his reappearance dressed as a young Apollo (Greek god of music and poetry). Euphorion represents poetry, especially Romantic poetry.

Lines 9679–9907
The best way to understand this extraordinary scene is as part of an opera. If you know *The Magic Flute*, by Wolfgang Amadeus Mozart, you will have a good idea of the effect Goethe intended. The music and the poetry themselves produce change, so that

it doesn't seem ridiculous but magical for a boy to
grow up, chase girls, and die all within the course
of a song.

Euphorion erupts on the stage like a dancing
star, whirling through the Chorus and pulling them
into a dance. He leaps up a mountain, carrying a
girl who proves to be the spirit of fire and who
entices him higher up the cliff. Helen and Faust
behave like all parents, worrying about a possible
fall, and they are deeply hurt when Euphorion
seems to be leaving them.

The climax comes as he reaches the top of the
cliff and spreads his clothes like wings. He falls,
but you don't see his twisted body. Everything
disappears, and only a pathetic heap of clothes
and a lyre are left behind. Euphorion's voice calls
to his mother, who is shattered, from the underworld, begging her not to leave him there alone.
The idyll is over.

NOTE: The fate of Euphorion (the name means
"agile one" or "light one") shows the tragedy
brought about by excess enthusiasm. He wants to
experience great passion, to fly away into the realm
of ideal beauty. This desire to fly really makes him
a son of Faust, who also wants to break free of the
restraints that a bodily, finite existence places on
the human spirit. Euphorion has the highest spiritual qualities of man—but he has no wings. Do
you think Goethe is saying that man has to be
content with life around him? That neither the
Classical nor the Romantic is sufficient by itself?
Remember that Goethe saw the universe as a whole
in which all aspects of being were related.

Some readers suggest that this scene represents

the process of poetic creation. Helen, Euphorion's mother, is timeless, and the child, who also represents poetry, is godlike and develops outside the usual course. Some readers argue that Euphorion's short and brilliant career symbolizes the spirit of poetry and its ability to make hearts lighter and lift mankind from its cares. Poetry concerns love and the flames of love. But as a human artifact, it cannot entirely escape human limitations. Like Icarus, the mythological figure who flew too near the sun, so that the wax holding his artificial wings together melted and he fell, the spirit of poetry falls when it defies its limitations. Euphorion is Goethe's tribute to Lord Byron (1788–1824), who exemplified the Romantic poet. Byron lived like Euphorion—committed to feeling, enthusiasm, and love—and died in Greece fighting for Greek independence from the Turks.

Lines 9908–10,008

Helen recognizes that her beauty once again has brought disaster after causing brief delight. She holds Faust in one last embrace, returns to the underworld, from which he had released her, and leaves only her robe and veil in his arms. These garments will allow Faust to leave this painful scene. Phorcyas tells him to hold onto the robe, which, dissolving into a cloud, lifts him and takes him away. In the next act you will find out where Faust goes.

The leader of the Chorus tries to persuade the women to follow her down into the underworld, where Helen has gone, but they aren't interested in being stuck behind Helen in Hades. They choose

instead to become part of nature. The first three
groups become nymphs of the trees, the mountains, and the river, while the last group becomes
nymphs of the vine and grapes.

With their speech, the tone changes. It is no
longer a song of mourning for the tragedy that has
just concluded, but takes on the faster rhythms
first of a wine pressing and then of a drunken revel.
The wine god, Dionysus, is greeted as the song
whirls to a climax. The curtain abruptly cuts off
the orgy. Mephistopheles reveals himself, throw-
ing off his Phorcyas disguise.

Think about the fact that Mephistopheles is the
last figure you see in the Helen Act. He certainly
played a similar role here as in the story of Gretchen,
pandering to Faust's desires, but to what extent?
What do you think caused the failure of Faust's
union with the most beautiful woman in the world?

ACT IV

HIGH MOUNTAINS

Lines 10,040–10,233
This scene parallels the first scene in Part II. The
devastation of a passionate love affair leaves a void,
a need for healing. Impelled by such a need, Faust
turns from love to public affairs, just as he did in
Act I, and becomes involved with the Emperor
again.

Faust is carried to the mountains of Germany by
the cloud that developed out of Helen's robe. He
looks at the clouds around him as they form shapes,
and sees first an imposing, "godlike female form"
whose majesty makes him remember the pleasures

he had recently enjoyed with Helen. The shape, however, soon disintegrates. It is replaced by a little cloud, which rises from vapor around Faust. The cloud represents Gretchen, his first love, "most cherished boon [favor] of earliest youth." You may be surprised at how deeply he still feels about her, for as the cloud dissipates he declares that it is taking with it "the best my soul contains." Women for Faust have now become mere shapes in the sky, heavenly beings that he can hardly recognize before they begin to float away. You will now see that Faust turns away from the quest for women, beauty, and idealism and turns toward practical matters.

Mephistopheles appears to see what Faust wants to do next. You may sometimes forget that Mephistopheles is Faust's servant, and that his power is at Faust's disposal. The two play a guessing game about Faust's desires. He wants power, but not the "hero's fame," which is all that Mephistopheles can think of. Notice that Faust, the true Romantic, says "the Deed is all." The Deed, in this instance, is the reclaiming of land from the sea, and he challenges Mephistopheles to help him.

NOTE: In the final two acts of *Faust*, you'll find Faust engaged in practical activities. Some readers believe that Goethe is suggesting that activity is man's natural element, that he is most likely to find satisfaction and fulfillment in work. What do you think?

Goethe, as an administrator at Weimar, had worked on schemes for the maximum use of land. He was also interested in tides and the movements

of bodies of water, as well as in geology. Why did
Goethe include the conversation betwen Mephistopheles and Faust regarding the origins of
mountains? Some believe that he was trying to develop the theme of order being created from chaos.
Is Faust's plan to reclaim land from the sea part of
that theme?

Notice the change in Faust. He is rejecting
Mephistopheles' suggestion that life should be filled
with pleasure, and he is planning a project that
requires work and that will accomplish good. Do
you think this change is a result of his experiences
in Greece and his exposure to noble ideals?

Faust is interrupted by the sounds of war behind
him, and the project is temporarily postponed.
Mephistopheles tells him that the Emperor has
squandered his kingdom's riches in personal
pleasures, and now he is facing rebellion by his
subjects, who want to be ruled by someone "who
can give us peace." Faust liked the Emperor for
his openness—expressing the Romantic admiration for honesty and sincerity of feeling. As they
set off to see the Emperor, Mephistopheles suggests a respectable motivation for helping the be-
leaguered ruler: If they can put the country on its
feet again, the people will support him again.

Now, however, he points out a second, self-
seeking motivation for helping the Emperor: If they
win the battle, then Faust can ask for the sea coast
that he wants to reclaim. Faust prefers Mephistopheles to fight the battle, saying that he has no
knowledge of military affairs. Mephistopheles as-
sures him that he will do the real work while Faust

carries the title of Generalissimo. He has already
made arrangements by bringing in the Three Mighty
Men (who fought with David and the Israelites
against the Philistines), apparently summoning
them from Hell.

NOTE: Allegorical figures, such as these three,
are not real characters as such, but representations
of the qualities suggested by their names. As
Mephistopheles presents each of them, they make
a speech displaying those qualities. Pugnacious
declares that he attacks before he's attacked; Ra-
pacious greedily goes for what he can steal; and
Tenacious hangs on to what he has. You may know
of other allegorical figures, such as the Seven Deadly
Sins in medieval plays. You certainly know our
national allegorical figure, the Statue of Liberty in
New York Harbor, who symbolizes, with her lamp,
the ideals of the United States. The three allegorical figures also represent a shift in Goethe's allusions. These figures share a biblical background.
You will notice that, in Acts IV and V, the number
of biblical references increases. In the original edi-
tion, they are marked in the margin with the appropriate name and number of the biblical chapter
and verse that Goethe used as his source.

Why does Goethe use so many biblical references in Act IV? Some readers say they function
as a commentary on the cooperation of earthly rulers
(the Emperor and his court) with the powers of
evil, represented by Mephistopheles. Is Goethe

suggesting that the rulers should be working with
God, but aren't?

IN THE FOOTHILLS

Lines 10,344–10,546
The Emperor prepares his army for battle and re-
ceives reports from his scouts. He learns that a
rival emperor is challenging his right to reign. The
Emperor reacts with bluster, declaring that he will
personally fight now that he has a rival. Faust must
have overheard these words as he entered with
the Three Mighty Men. He offers the Emperor the
assistance of magic, but the Emperor still wants to
fight his rival. Faust argues against his desire to
fight in person, and the Emperor agrees. The Emperor's decision gives Faust an opportunity to as-
sign his three allegorical figures to the battle array.

Lines 10,547–10,782
When Mephistopheles first appears, he says that
he has summoned a phantom army of old armor
to make a fearful noise that will frighten the enemy
forces of the rival emperor. But the enemy isn't
falling back. Instead, it is beginning to advance
toward the watching group. Even Mephistopheles
is afraid.

Defeat seems so certain that the commander-in-
chief resigns his office, and the Emperor seems to
give up completely. Left to themselves, Faust and
Mephistopheles arrange a dubious victory by magically flooding the mountainsides and then frightening the enemy with lightning in the bushes. The
empty armor that Mephistopheles conjured up now
joins in, as the battle becomes a victory for the
Emperor's forces.

NOTE: This scene is important because it places
the Emperor in Faust's debt. It also seems to suggest that even destructive forces, such as the evil
magic of Mephistopheles, can, through wise and
systematic planning, be used for good purposes.
The qualities represented by the Three Mighty Men
can be useful if they are organized and used
wisely.

As the victorious troops carry off gold from the
defeated emperor's tent, the Emperor enters and
begins appointing new officers for his court. His
speeches betray his vanity and self-deception. He
believes the victory was achieved by his soldiers,
and the flood was only a chance happening.

In this final scene of Act IV, the last person the
Emperor talks to is the Archbishop. Like the Chancellor in the first scene with the Emperor, the
Archbishop knows that the Emperor has been
working with the Devil. Because the Archbishop
is always looking to increase the Church's prop-
erties and revenue, he plays on the Emperor's guilt
feelings. The Emperor can buy his way back into
the Church's good graces if he gives it the foothill
land where the battle was fought and where the
Emperor accepted help from Mephistopheles and
Faust. A cathedral will be built on this site.

The Archbishop's parting shot concerns the land
for which Faust and Mephistopheles had inter-
vened in the battle. The Archbishop demands the
income from that land for the Church. The Emperor, however, now becomes annoyed with the
Archbishop's persistent demands and angrily de-

clares that the land isn't even there—it's under water. Goethe's perception of the Church as greedy seems to be evident here. Remember that the Church accepted from Gretchen's mother the first casket of jewels that Mephistopheles and Faust had left in Gretchen's room.

Is greed Faust's motive for intervention in the Emperor's war? What has happened to the Faust who was a suitable partner for Helen? Has he been so disappointed in his striving for the sublime that he has given up and decided to pursue practical matters? Or is he simply progressing from experience with love to experience with power?

And what about Mephistopheles? Is he losing his grip on Faust and on his magic powers? Some readers believe that in Part II, Mephistopheles becomes subordinate to Faust, but others think Act IV shows that Mephistopheles is dominating Faust so much that Faust is losing his moral sense. Do you agree with either of these views?

ACT V
OPEN COUNTRY

The first scene creates a mood that will contrast sharply with the following scene. The first words describe a welcoming tree, which shelters a small cottage where Baucis and Philemon live a humble but completely contented old age.

Goethe chose Baucis and Philemon to become victims of Faust's ambition in Act IV because he expected his audience to recognize and be sympathetic toward them. The story of Baucis and Philemon, taken from Greek mythology, also appears in the *Metamorphoses*—a collection of myths and legends about changes of form—by the Roman poet Ovid (43 B.C.–A.D. 17). Baucis and Philemon are a devoted old couple who are so kind to some visitors—gods in disguise—that when they die the gods change them into two trees with intertwined limbs. They remain together eternally, a symbol of marital happiness.

The old couple entertain a young traveler whom they had rescued from the sea earlier in their lives. Philemon explains to the traveler that much of the land around them used to be under water—the first hint that Faust's reclamation scheme has succeeded. Faust first lived by his new land in "tents and huts," but now he has a palace. Baucis suspects that her new neighbor relied on unnatural powers. She doesn't trust Faust, who by now has become powerful, but Philemon believes a promise he made to give them a homestead on the reclaimed land. They walk together to the chapel, trusting in God to protect them.

PALACE

You may find it hard to like Faust in this scene. He is now old (Goethe said in a letter that he was one hundred years old) and apparently has everything he wants—a palace on his reclaimed land and ships bringing riches along the canal to his docks. But he wants his land to be perfect, and it can't be while Baucis and Philemon live in their little hut and the bell peals in their chapel. The innocent and peaceful lives of Baucis and Philemon make Faust uneasy. They represent a natural life (symbolized by their living on "original" or

unreclaimed land and by the church bells) in which
Faust can't participate. He seems to think his
uneasiness will disappear once he has their land.

Mephistopheles and the Three Mighty Men bring
in their cargo, but Faust doesn't react with any
welcoming pleasure. Mephistopheles, who is in-
sensitive to human striving, tries to persuade Faust
that he has achieved his aim. Faust bursts in with
his complaint that the hut and the chapel are spoil-
ing his view. He can't stand the tinkling of the bell.
Baucis and Philemon must be removed to a "hand-
some little farm" he had assigned them earlier.
Mephistopheles whistles up the Three Mighty Men
and off they go to evict Baucis and Philemon.

DEEP NIGHT

This is an intensely dramatic scene, including,
in a very few lines, pathos and irony to break the
heart. The horrified watchman, at the top of the
palace, reports that the hut and the chapel are on
fire. Faust, grumbling at the watchman's cries, looks
forward to sitting on a platform where the burnt
tree now stands and being able to look down on
the farm of Baucis and Philemon.

Mephistopheles shatters Faust's dream with a
story of casual cruelty that will remind you of his
attitude toward Gretchen's sufferings. The old
people died of fright when they were awakened
by Mephistopheles and the Three Mighty Men, who
killed the traveler in a scuffle that caused the fire.

Faust curses them and blames his own thought-
lessness. He stares miserably at the burned cottage
and chapel, as four spirits form themselves in the
smoke. This is a major change for Faust. He is

sorry for what has happened and accepts responsibility for it, even though he hadn't intended to
destroy Baucis and Philemon. Contrast this with
his reluctance to accept responsibility for Gretch-
en's ruin in Part I.

NOTE: What happened to Baucis and Philemon
is tragically familiar to us—think of villages sub-
merged for hydroelectric dams, illnesses and death
caused by insecticides and herbicides, the threat
of nuclear holocaust. Some readers downplay the
pathos of Baucis and Philemon, regarding such in-
cidents as inevitable in the careers of "supermen"
like Faust. The word "superman" here refers to an
important concept in German philosophy and political thought. A superman is a figure who fear-
lessly endeavors to achieve his ends, disregarding
the suffering his actions may cause others, whom
he considers inferior and of little consequence in
the great scheme of things.

MIDNIGHT

The spirits have become four allegorical figures—Want, Debt, Need, and Care. The first three
cannot enter a rich man's house, but Care slips
through the keyhole. The others see Death approaching Faust's palace.

Faust must be aware that he is approaching the
end of his life, because he begins summarizing it
in a dialogue with Care. He realizes that he is still
obligated to Mephistopheles and other supernatural forces who have helped him, such as the Three
Mighty Men. He understands that he is not a free

man if he must depend on super-human help. He also reveals that he thinks man should only worry about what is attainable and not concern himself too much with what he can't have. Because he is so dependent on technology, modern man is sometimes described as "Faustian." How valid do you think this description is?

NOTE: Care is presented as an old hag determined to ruin Faust's last hours. You may think she personifies Faust's conscience regarding what has happened to Baucis and Philemon. Many readers have argued for that interpretation. If that's all she is, then Faust's speech makes him look callous. But you can look at Care in a different light. Care is much like anxiety, which can demoralize man and destroy his will. When man's will is destroyed, he stops striving, and when man stops striving, he is finished.

Faust, however, doesn't give in to Care, so she avenges herself by blinding him and making him taste—at the end of his life—the sufferings he has avoided. But blindness doesn't stop Faust. It seems like another challenge, something for him to strive against as he has all his life. He calls for workmen to continue a new project he has in mind. His final words in this scene show how much value he places on his intellectual powers.

GREAT OUTER PRECINCT OF THE PALACE

This is Faust's death scene. You know it before Faust does, because Mephistopheles is supervising a crew digging his grave. The creatures who do the work are "lemures," classical spirits of the evil dead. As they dig, the blind Faust mistakes the noise for work on the project he mentioned at the end of the previous scene.

He dies with a vision of technological achievement before his eyes—a drained swamp made into fertile farmland. At the moment of his death, he says that the sight of such an achievement would have fulfilled him, for he would have wanted the moment to be eternal: "Tarry yet, thou art so fair!" But such "high happiness" is still to come.

And so Mephistopheles has lost his bet. Faust has never actually said that he wants a moment to continue, never attained his "striving's crown and sum." Mephistopheles acknowledges his defeat in a bitterly negative speech.

ENTOMBMENT

Goethe shows his genius as a dramatist here in making the fight for Faust's soul into broad comedy. Parts of this scene come from the old Faust stories, where the gaping mouth of Hell struck terror into the audience at the end of the play. But the best part, where Mephistopheles is distracted by the nakedness of the young angels, is Goethe's invention.

Mephistopheles thinks he'll seize Faust's soul as it slips away from the body, so he brings up all the paraphernalia of Hell, complete with fat and lean devils. He arranges them around the corpse, so that they can catch the soul as it flies up.

NOTE: In the original Faust stories, Faust is dragged off to Hell at the end as Mephistopheles claims his soul. These stories warned Christians not to strive for more knowledge than a man should have. The gaping Hell mouth and the devils with pitchforks were designed to frighten the spectators into following the Church's teaching. But Goethe's *Faust* does not convey a Christian moral. Mephistopheles does not win Faust's "immortal essence," because Faust was never so satisfied with the results of his striving that he wanted time to stand still. Mephistopheles can only seize Faust's soul by a trick, since he never turned Faust away from the "right way" (you'll remember these words from the Prologue in Heaven).

A cloud of angels, surrounded by heavenly light, begins to sing, to Mephistopheles' intense scorn. They strew rose petals, which send the devils back to Hell, and burn Mephistopheles' skin where they fall on him. The angels warn him that he cannot have Faust's soul, for it does not rightfully belong to him. Then they lure him to the side by making themselves so sexually attractive he can't help gazing at them. The angels are exquisite young boys, and Mephistopheles loses his head.

Just as Mephistopheles realizes that a trick is being played on him, the chorus of angels seizes Faust's immortal part and rises to Heaven with it. Mephistopheles curses himself for his "vulgar lust, absurd amours," although he recognizes the immense power of sexual love: "No mean folly it must be."

MOUNTAIN GORGES

The final scene of the drama has puzzled readers since the second part of *Faust* was published in 1832. Why did Goethe choose traditional Christian symbolism to end a work that does not follow Christian doctrine? What does it mean for Faust's soul to be "saved"? Why do women carry Faust's soul into Heaven?

Your reading of *Faust* will suggest some answers. Some readers believe that the scene serves only as a kind of balance to the Prologue in Heaven, and that it shouldn't be taken too seriously. Others believe that Goethe used Christian symbolism as an answer to the original Faust legend: Yes, the original Faust was dragged off to Hell; but this Faust, who represents mankind, is taken to Heaven, because he has won his wager with the Devil. Still others argue that Goethe believed man couldn't save himself, so he used Christian symbols to represent a higher force than man. He may have used Christian symbols because he knew they would be readily understood by his audience.

This scene brings together several of the themes of *Faust*. Faust's soul is carried upward across a landscape of wild beauty. You will recognize the significance of the natural background—Nature is almost like a religion for Goethe. The Anchorite Fathers—Pater Ecstaticus, Pater Profundus, Pater Seraphicus, and Doctor Marianus represent the mystical tradition of early Christianity, which Goethe learned to admire from Herder. (In the Roman Catholic Church, St. Anthony, c. 250–c. 350, was known as *ecstaticus*; St. Bernard, 1091–1153, as *profundus;* and St. Francis of Assisi, 1182–1226, as *seraphicus.*)

Despite its emotional intensity, this scene is not solemn. It is full of joy. The Blessed Boys represent the freedom of innocence, unwilling to be bound to earth. They fly up toward the angels, who bear Faust's "immortal essence," which they have snatched from Mephistopheles by the trick they describe with obvious pleasure.

The first chorus of angels is important for the meaning of the whole drama. The angels' song explains that Faust's special status as the equal of spiritual beings like Helen, and his ceaseless striving, have guaranteed him salvation. But he will be welcomed to Heaven also because "transfigured love" has spoken on his behalf. This refers to Gretchen, who loved Faust deeply—too deeply for her own good—and was redeemed.

As the angels life Faust's soul upward, they pass it on to the Blessed Boys, who give it a new beginning. Then Doctor Marianus sings a hymn of praise to the Virgin Mary as the mystical ideal of woman. He describes the chorus of penitent women who are asking for the Virgin Mary's help to be saved.

The three penitent women of Christian tradition join in pleading for the forgiveness of Gretchen's sin as she joins them, singing a version of the prayer she spoke in her despair by the city wall. As the Blessed Boys describe how Faust's soul will grow so that he can become their teacher, Gretchen begs the Virgin Mary to allow her to lead his soul into salvation.

Her prayer is granted. Gretchen is told to fly upward and Faust will follow her. The drama ends

with a beautiful general chorus in praise of "Woman
Eternal." The chorus announces that in Heaven
man finds what was unattainable on earth: understanding, action, sincerity. After his long and troubled journey, Faust is at rest, redeemed by the love
of women.

A STEP BEYOND

Tests and Answers
TESTS

Test 1

1. Goethe changed the traditional Faust legend   ____
   by
   - I. having Faust fall in love with a young
     maiden, Gretchen
   - II. allowing Faust to find redemption at
     the end of the drama
   - III. bringing in the episode of Helen of
     Troy from Greek mythology
   - A. I and III only   B. I and II only
   - C. I, II, and III

2. *Faust* was written   ____
   - A. in the last twenty years of Goethe's
     life
   - B. during his Italian visit, 1786–88
   - C. on and off throughout sixty years of
     his life

3. The Lord says that Mephistopheles   ____
   - A. has no place in the universe
   - B. keeps man on the move
   - C. is the jester in Heaven

4. Faust is prevented from committing suicide   ____
   by the
   - A. entrance of Wagner

B. movements of the poodle
C. sound of the church bells ringing for
Easter

5. In the Witches' Kitchen, Faust   _____
    I. drinks a magic potion
   II. sees a beautiful woman in a magic
       mirror
  III. steps into a magic circle
   A. I and II only   B. II and III only
   C. I, II, and III

6. At the Walpurgis Night, Faust remembers   _____
   Gretchen because
   A. an apparition resembling Gretchen
      appears with a red line around her
      throat
   B. a red mouse jumps from the mouth of
      a witch he's dancing with
   C. he falls asleep and dreams

7. The Emperor signs the document author-   _____
   izing paper money
   A. in council with his ministers
   B. when he appears as Pan in the
      Carnival masque
   C. when Mephistopheles gives it to him

8. Faust is shown the entrance to the under- _____
   world by
   A. Chiron   B. Homunculus
   C. Manto

9. Using only Faust's monologues, trace Faust's journey through life.

10. In what ways is the relationship between Faust and Mephistopheles different at the end of Part II from what it was at the beginning, in Part I?

11. Contrast the Walpurgis Night in Part I with the Classical Walpurgis Night in Part II.

Test 2

1. Romanticism is identified with   ——
   A. feeling, folk poetry, the gloomy North
   B. order, aristocracy, Italy and Greece
   C. reasoned thought

2. Goethe imitated the verse forms of   ——
   I. Shakespeare
   II. Dante
   III. Euripides
   A. I and II only   B. II and III only
   C. I, II, and III

3. Mephistopheles will get Faust's soul when   ——
   A. Faust dies without the last rites of the Church
   B. Faust says to a moment of fulfillment, "Stay! thou art so fair!"
   C. he has served Faust for twenty-four years

4. Gretchen takes the second gift of jewels to   ——
   Martha's house because
   A. she has stolen them
   B. Mephistopheles told her to
   C. her mother gave the first jewels to the Church

5. Homunculus is born in his test tube when   ——
   A. Mephistopheles enters the laboratory

B. Wagner shakes the test tube
C. Faust dreams of his birth

6. Euphorion is compared to   _____
    I. Icarus
    II. Lord Byron
    III. Galatea
    A. I and III only   B. I and II only
    C. I, II, and III

7. Mephistopheles disguises himself as one of   _____
    the Phorcyads, who are the
    A. Furies   B. Fates   C. Graeae

8. The Emperor must build a cathedral for the   _____
    Archbishop because
    A. the rival emperor won the battle
    B. he promised land to Faust
    C. he used the Devil's power to defeat
        his rival

9. Contrast the Faust you first meet in his study and
    the Faust who dies, blind and old. How has he
    changed and how has he remained the same?

10. How does Faust's relationship to Gretchen differ from
    his relationship to Helen?

11. Faust speaks of "two souls in my breast." Illustrate
    how the theme of conflict is expressed in *Faust*.

ANSWERS

Test 1
1. B   2. C   3. B   4. C   5. C   6. A
7. B   8. C

9. Make a list of Faust's monologues and characterize each one briefly. The first takes place in the opening scene. Faust is dissatisfied with his knowledge, tries to raise the Earth Spirit, is rejected, and falls into such despair that he almost commits suicide. This is basic information for your answer, the beginning of Faust's journey. The second monologue occurs in Forest and Cave, where Faust thanks the Earth Spirit for giving him the opportunity to experience life fully. Clearly, Faust's journey has taken him toward sensual satisfaction. The third great monologue opens Part II, in Charming Landscape. Now Faust is recovering from the horrors of Gretchen's death and his infinite guilt. Where is he in his life's journey at this point? He certainly isn't buoyant, as he was in Forest and Cave, and he isn't expressing the dissatisfaction he felt in the opening scene. He has become a man who understands experience deeply because he has lived through terrible events. During the monologue, he elaborates a metaphor that enables him to forgive himself and continue his journey. You will need to explain the metaphor in some detail.

The monologue at the beginning of Act IV is again the expression of deep sorrow about a woman, this time Helen of Troy. It is a renunciation of women. Faust's final speech alone occurs after Care has blinded him and left him apparently helpless. It is a speech full of desperate energy, urging workmen to complete what he has planned. What kind of journey is charted by these monologues? It doesn't seem to be a smooth one. Can it be characterized as universal, a path taken by all men?

10. Make a list of the scenes in which Faust and Mephistopheles appear together and summarize what happens in each. Are they polite to each other? Characterize the terms in which they speak to each other, from

Mephistopheles' embarrassment at being unable to leave Faust's study, through Faust's bitter accusations in the prose scene and Mephistopheles' sending Faust down to the Mothers, to the remarks Mephistopheles makes under his breath as Faust, blind, dies. Does the relationship deteriorate or remain about the same? If it changes, is it Faust who changes his attitude or Mephistopheles? You should answer the question in your first paragraph and then support it with specific references and quotations.

11. Write down the main features of the Walpurgis Night in Part I. It's held on a high mountain, the Brocken, which Faust and Mephistopheles climb by the uncertain light of a Will-o'-the-Wisp. They visit groups of witches sitting around fires and dance with them, until Faust is reminded of Gretchen. The atmosphere is lurid, gloomy, evil. Then look at the Classical Walpurgis Night for the same features: Since this time Faust is transported by Homunculus, there are three visitors to this Walpurgis Night, not two, led by Homunculus' brilliant light. Mephistopheles was in charge of the first Walpurgis Night, but here he is out of his element. The celebrations range over a wide landscape, concluding in the sea—exactly the opposite of the Brocken—with a ceremony of great beauty, as Galatea leads a procession and Homunculus smashes his test tube on her shell. There is also an intellectual discussion of the origins of life between Thales and Anaxagoras. What do all these differences mean? What general statement can you make about them that illuminates the meaning of the poem?

Test 2

1. A   2. A   3. B   4. C   5. A   6. B
7. C   8. C

9. This question asks you to estimate whether experiences have made any difference to Faust. First, characterize him when you first see him in his study. He's deeply dissatisfied with his knowledge, given to sharp mood swings, despairing to the point of suicide but obviously ready and able to command Mephistopheles. Look at his relations with Wagner, the peasants, and Mephistopheles. Then, using that information, contrast Faust in the final scenes of the play. Is he still suicidal? If not, how would you characterize his reaction to the misfortune of blindness? Is he now concerned with knowledge or with action? How do his relationships differ, especially to Mephistopheles? If you find that he has changed a great deal, you'll have to consider whether he's recognizably the same person. Would you characterize the changes as improvements in character? Did you like or admire Faust more at the beginning of the drama or at the end?

10. It's fairly easy to describe Faust's relationship to Gretchen, at least at first. Clearly, he wants to have sexual relations with her, and that's about all. He has an intense feeling for her, but it's limited—it isn't enough to stop him from going off with Mephistopheles and forgetting all about her. The problem arises when he finds out what has happened to her. How guilty does he feel—and how responsible? Is his desire to release her from prison a genuine attempt to rescue her or only another gush of feeling?

His relationship to Helen is different in almost every way. It isn't a simple, sexual passion but the adoration of an ideal. Helen isn't real—both she and Faust's relationship with her are mythical, existing in the world of imagination. Their whole story takes place in one scene, consisting of their marriage, the birth and death of Eu-

phorion, their son, and Helen's return to the underworld. Their love-making begins as Faust teaches Helen
about rhyme, uncommon in Greek literature. What significance does this have?

At first glance, you would think that the two relationships are similar, in that both end in failure. But look
more closely and you'll see how different the failures
are. The failure of the relationship with Gretchen is an
old story: Such relationships end in disaster—or shot-
gun marriages. But the marrige with Helen cannot last,
because it symbolizes an impossible union, between the
Romantic and the Classical spirits. It is a failure on a
completely different level.

11. Look first at the "two souls" passage. What are the
two souls, or yearnings, agitating Faust? Faust tells
Wagner that he is torn between the world of human
action, with all its sensual pleasures, and the world of
pure intellect, which soars above earthly concerns. One
immediate expression of the conflict is right in front of
you—Wagner represents the first world and Faust the
second. Then, start looking for other conflicts embodied
in the play. Faust both depends upon and cannot tolerate Mephistopheles—a conflict that represents his desire for experience pitted against the unpleasantness of
doing what he must do to get it. There are conflicts
between the solitude of Faust's study and the bustling
town full of people celebrating Easter Day, between Word
and Deed, between darkness and light. It is even possible to say that the "two souls" represent the Classical
and Romantic styles that alternate throughout *Faust*. Can
you pull all these, as well as any other examples, together and make a general statement about the "two
souls" image as a central idea in the poem?

Term Paper Ideas and other Topics for Writing

The Characters

1. Is Faust the hero of *Faust*? Explain.

2. Write a character study of Mephistopheles.

3. What does *Faust* tell you about students in German universities in Faust's day?

4. Describe the heavenly characters in *Faust*—the Lord, the angels, and the other inhabitants of Heaven.

5. What are Faust's religious beliefs?

6. Write a character study of Homunculus.

7. Why did the Emperor assume the role of Pan in the Carnival masque? What does that indicate about his character?

8. Compare Gretchen, Martha, and Lieschen (the girl at the well in Part I).

Literary Topics

1. What is the meaning of natural elements such as fire, water, and light in *Faust*?

2. What is the meaning of gold and money in *Faust*?

3. Describe and analyze each of the settings in the drama. Explain how each contributes to the ideals expressed and to the telling of the Faust story.

4. What dreams do you find in *Faust*? Who dreams them? What do they mean?

5. What is the significance of churches, cathedrals, and the sound of bells in *Faust*?

6. Goethe is remarkable for his sense imagery. Find examples of this in *Faust* and discuss how the images enhance the meaning of the passages you've chosen.

7. How does Goethe's *Faust* differ from Marlowe's *Tragedy of Doctor Faustus*?

8. Charles Gounod composed an opera based on the Faust story. How does the opera differ from Goethe's play?

Philosophy

1. Can you draw a moral from *Faust*? Does it tell us how to conduct our lives? Explain.

2. Faust wants to translate the first line of the Gospel of St. John to read, "In the beginning was the *Deed*." Discuss this as an example of Romantic theory, with its applications in the poem.

3. Is *Faust* a Classical or a Romantic work?

4. Explain why Goethe uses Christian symbolism in *Faust*.

5. In what sense is Mephistopheles the Lord's servant?

Further Reading
BIOGRAPHICAL WORKS

Angelloz, Joseph-François. *Goethe*. Translated by R. H. Blackley. New York: Orion, 1958.

Goethe, Johann Wolfgang. *Autobiography*. Translated by John Oxenford. New York: Horizon, 1969.

————. *Conversations with Eckermann*. Translated by John Oxenford. Berkeley: North Point Press, 1984.

Van Abbe, Derek. *Goethe: New Perspectives on a Writer and His Time*. London: Allen & Unwin, 1972.

CRITICAL WORKS

Atkins, Stuart. *Goethe's Faust: A Literary Criticism.* Cambridge, Mass.: Harvard University Press, 1964. An exhaustive, scholarly line-by-line commentary.

Cottrell, Alan P. *Goethe's Faust: Seven Essays.* Chapel Hill: University of North Carolina Press, 1976. Examines the themes of *Faust* and relates them to the modern era.

Enright, D. J. *Commentary on Goethe's Faust.* New York: New Directions, 1949. A provocative personal statement, the most radical of those who devalue Part II in favor of Part I.

Fairley, Barker. *Goethe's Faust: Six Essays.* Oxford: Clarendon, 1953. Offers valuable insight into the play.

Gearey, John. *Goethe's Faust: The Making of Part I.* New Haven: Yale University Press, 1981. Treats *Faust* as a masterpiece of world literature, focusing on it as a work of art rather than a philosophical poem.

Gillies, Alexander. *Goethe's Faust: An Interpretation.* Oxford: Blackwell, 1957. A thought-provoking commentary, but quoted passages are not translated.

Jantz, Harold. *The Form of Faust.* Baltimore: Johns Hopkins, 1978. Concentrates on *Faust* as a literary work.

Lange, Victor, ed. *Goethe: A Collection of Critical Essays.* Englewood Cliffs: Prentice-Hall, 1968. Essays on Goethe's writings, including examinations of poetic expression and the problem of unity and form in *Faust.*

Mann, Thomas. "Goethe's *Faust,*" in *Essays by Thomas Mann.* New York: Vintage, 1958. A perceptive, personal appreciation of Goethe's play.

Mason, Eudo C. *Goethe's Faust: Its Genesis and Purport.* Los Angeles: University of California Press, 1967. Scholarly discussion, heavily weighted in favor of Part I over Part II.

TRANSLATIONS OF *FAUST*

Arndt, Walter. *Faust: A New Translation.* Edited by Cyrus Hamlin. New York: Norton, 1976. A verse translation, with notes, critical essays, and background and sources.

Fairley, Barker. *Goethe's Faust.* Toronto: University of Toronto, 1970. Prose translation.

Jarrell, Randall. *Goethe's Faust, Part I.* New York: Farrar, Straus, & Giroux, 1959. Verse translation.

MacIntyre, Carlyle F. *Goethe's Faust.* Norfolk, Connecticut: New Directions, 1941. Verse translation with facing text; illustrations by Rockwell Kent.

MacNiece, Louis. *Goethe's Faust.* Oxford: Oxford University Press, 1951.

Raphael, Alice. *Faust, Part I.* New York: Heritage Club, n.d. Verse translation, illustrated with eighteen lithographs by Delacroix.

Wayne, Philip. *Faust, Part I* and *Faust, Part II.* 2 vols. New York: Penguin, 1949. Verse translation.

AUTHOR'S OTHER MAJOR WORKS

1773   *Götz von Berlichingen,* a play about a
        medieval German knight.

1774   *The Sorrows of Young Werther,* a novel.

1787   *Iphigenie in Tauris,* a play.

1788   *Egmont,* a play.

1789   *Torquato Tasso,* a play.

1796   *Wilhelm Meister's Apprenticeship,* a novel.

1809   *Elective Affinities,* a novel.

1811   *Poetry and Truth,* an autobiographical work.

1818   *West-East Divan,* a collection of lyrics.

1821   *Wilhelm Meister's Years of Travel,* a novel.

The Critics

On the Meaning of *Faust*

For after all it is a poem and not just a moral dis-
course—a poem which, more boldly perhaps than
any in the modern era, attempts to convey what
life is like, not, to be sure, in all its characteristics,
but in some of them, as they appeared at a great
moment in history. It so happens that Goethe came
at a time in Europe when there was a great up-
surge of life. European society after a period of
premature stability broke its bounds, emotionally,
intellectually, and politically, and underwent a great
expansion, the consequences of which we are still
discovering. It was the spirit of this expansion, and
the sense of energy and initiative that accom-
panied it in its first stages, that Goethe's *Faust*
managed to capture and to set down in imperish-
able language.

The result is a poem unlike all other great poems
in its confidence in man, man's self-reliance, his
capacity for growth, his future. It is true that Faust
has his mistakes, his exasperations, his despairs.
But these are incidental and subordinate to the
poem's unquenchable optimism. What has ap-
pealed to past generations in this poem is its reso-
nance, its potential, its affirmation of life, and this
is what will appeal again to generations to come.

—Barker Fairley, *Goethe's Faust: Six
Essays,* 1953

On Helen

This Helen is not the dream Helen of the Imperial
palace. She is real, real in the sense that she takes
part in the dramatic action, just as any other character does. She lives in Greek surroundings, uses
authentic Greek metres and has a Greek chorus to
accompany her. Moreover, she feels herself to be
real and speaks of prosaic everyday events (even of
seasickness) in a practical way. It is only when Faust

and Mephistopheles intervene that her reality is impaired and she is forced out of her native epoch and steps into another. Modern man, if he wishes to consort with antiquity, can only do so by incorporating it into his own age.

—Alexander Gillies, *Goethe's Faust:
An Interpretation*, 1957

On Mephistopheles

Mephisto has baffled more than one admirer, notably Schiller, for he is a complex figure who borrows his many traits from Christianity, from the Faustian legend, from Lucifer and Ahriman (hardly understood by Goethe), from the poet himself, or from his friends Behrisch and Merck, perhaps even from Herder. In the "Forest and Cave" scene, he is an envoy of the "Spirit of the Earth." . . . He is the absence of faith, of trust, of love and of enthusiasm; he is ironic and sarcastic criticism; he is paralyzing reason; he is delight in destruction, perversions; he is the imperfection inherent in man and his works; he is Gretchen's death, the ugliness of the Phorkyade, the destruction of the house where Baucis and Philemon perish. Yet if he did not exist, man could not fulfill his earthly mission.

—Joseph-François Angelloz,
Goethe, 1958

On Gretchen

It is remarkable that even the most important point in the Gretchen tragedy, Faust's desertion of Gretchen, is only implied and nowhere directly presented or even mentioned. Some critics, especially those who think Faust should be regarded as an ideal, exemplary superman, have even tried to make out a case for his never having in the strict sense of the word deserted her at all.

—Eudo C. Mason, *Goethe's Faust:
Its Genesis and Purport*, 1967

CPSIA information can be obtained at www.ICGtesting.com
Printed in the USA
LVOW081952220113

316782LV00003B/219/A

9 780764 191091